P9-CCA-003

THE
JAMES BOND
TRIVIA QUIZ BOOK

THE
JAMES BOND
TRIVIA QUIZ BOOK

by
PHILIP GURIN

398 PRIAM BOOKS
ARBOR HOUSE
NEW YORK

Copyright © 1984 by Philip Gurin

All rights reserved, including the right of reproduction in whole or in part in any form. Published in the United States of America by Arbor House Publishing Company and in Canada by Fitzhenry & Whiteside, Ltd.

ISBN: 0-87795-580-8

Manufactured in the United States of America

10 9 8 7 6 5 4 3 2 1

ACKNOWLEDGMENTS

This book represents the combined knowledge of dozens of people, all of whom had the kindness and patience to assist me in my never-ending quest for fascinating and obscure facts about James Bond. To his fans, the world of James Bond is wonderfully full of facts, figures, production notes and peculiar details. To the uninitiated, 007 is nothing more than a cardboard automaton whose motion pictures happen to make big bucks. Of necessity, a book of this nature brings both groups together, and I found it a rewarding challenge to be working with both fans and non-fans alike.

An acknowledgments page means nothing of course to those whose names are not on it. Yet without the following people, this book would never have come to pass. So, here goes. . . .

First off, without the initial "zetz" given this project by a very good friend, Lisa Kovitz, this book would still be after-dinner conversation. For all that's happened, I owe her a special note of thanks.

For pictures, I must thank Stan Friedman at United Press International, Morris L. Hallowell IV at Aston Martin Lagonda of North America, Inc., Don Griffin at Perry Oceanographics, Lisa Bain at *Esquire* magazine, Mary Beth Whelan at Globe Photos, Michalle S. Belson at Revell Inc., Christine Duffy at Reeves International, Robert H. Magee at Interarms, Andrea Reitmayr at Sygma Photo News, Patricia Landis at Wide World Photos, Ivy Orta at Columbia Pictures and Stuart R. Kaplan at U.S. Games System.

For additional picture and information assistance, Richard Schenkman of the James Bond Fan Club, Ursula Andress, David Hedison, Clifton James, George Lazenby and Kristina Wayborn all have my sincerest appreciation, as does Film Historian's Jim Shoenberger, the folks at Jerry Ohlinger's Movie Material Store and Charlotte Wilson of the Independent Broadcasting Authority in London.

For their assistance, information, support and generosity, the following individuals deserve a special note of thanks: Gary Cee; Adam Chinitz; Graham Flashner; Eric Frankel; Michael Gill; Ronald, Shirley and Robin Gurin; De'lois Jacobs; Eleanor Johnson; Bob LaGuardia; Brad LaRosa; John McDaid; John Mura; Jerry Seaman Glenn Treibitz; Mitchell Waters; and the staff at the New York Public Library's Lincoln Center Clipping Collection.

For his help, good counsel and general "Godfathering," a special note of thanks and appreciation to Owen Laster at William Morris.

And finally, my deepest thanks to my beloved Cheryl, without whose patience, love and "tea and sympathy" this book could not have been written. For someone who was not much of a James Bond enthusiast, she now knows more about Agent 007 than she ever, in her wildest dreams, imagined she would.

CONTENTS

INTRODUCTION

More than one billion people have seen the films of James Bond, Agent 007 of Her Majesty's Secret Service. Over 42 million copies of Ian Fleming's books are in print. The James Bond movies have been rerun countless times on television and movie screens around the world, and the videotapes for home viewing are perennial bestsellers. At least five theme songs have become hit pop records, and scores of merchandising—from beer cans to raincoats–have been tied in to the inimitable Mr. Bond. Yet never has there been, in one volume, a collection of questions and answers about the world's most famous super spy.

Until now.

Included here are over 60 photographs and 500 questions and answers, ranging from the simple "Who played Miss Moneypenny?" to the most esoteric "What film caused riots in Boston?" to the utterly ridiculous "How many women has 007 kissed?"

The book is divided into 34 different quizzes, and addresses the movies, the books, production notes and historical background on James Bond. The movies are included in chronological order, and each film quiz contains questions relevant to the book or short story on which it was based. The answers, which can be found on pages 175–246, provide additional background information.

You can start at the beginning and work your way through to the end, or flip around and pick out random questions that test your knowledge of particular films or stories, or pick a quiz and answer all the questions on that topic. However you want to do it, you are sure to know more when you've finished this book than you did when you started.

Many people helped put this book together. Countless articles, magazines, clippings, microfilms, photos, books, screenings and many trivia experts were consulted. Unfortunately, I alone must take responsibility for any errors that may have crept through. Every effort has been made to check and double-check each answer, however, so the chances of a mistake slipping through are similar to those of Blofeld's getting away with murder (or Miss Moneypenny's spending an intimate evening with Mr. Bond).

Read and enjoy, laugh and learn. May this teaser into the world of 007 be as interesting and entertaining to read as it was to write.

—Phil Gurin
November 1983

1 IN THE BEGINNING

1) Ian Fleming began writing *CASINO ROYALE* on the third Tuesday of January in 1952. This James Bond novel was the first in what would prove to be one of the most successful literary series of all time. Why, at the age of 43, did Fleming start writing this book?
   A) He wanted to get out of the investment business.
   B) He was tired of working as a reporter.
   C) He was always fascinated with spy stories and thought he could write a better one.
   D) He was fighting premarital jitters.

IAN FLEMING, creator of James Bond, Agent 007

(CREDIT: UPI)

2) Fleming took the name of his famous hero from
   A) thin air. It came to him while playing bridge with his friend
   and neighbor, Noel Coward.
   B) a book about local birds of the West Indies.
   C) the telephone book for Jamaica, West Indies, where he lived
   in the hamlet of Oracabessa. He was subsequently sued for
   invasion of privacy by the real-life James Bond, who was
   finally forced to change his name to avoid further harass-
   ment.
   D) a maitre d' at the London pub Fleming frequented during his
   days as a Reuter's reporter.

3) Where did he get the idea to use the "double O" code for his
   "licensed to kill" department?
   A) He made it up.
   B) It was his lucky number at the roulette wheel.
   C) It was the number used by Whitehall to classify top secret
   documents.
   D) It was suggested to him by his friend, General "Wild Bill"
   Donovan, with whom he helped write the original CIA char-
   ter.

4) The name of Fleming's private beach house in Jamaica was
   A) Goldenrod
   B) Goldeneye
   C) Piz Gloria
   D) Xanadu

5) What is "Glidrose"?
   A) a flower
   B) Fleming's London townhouse
   C) part of a sugar, rum and insurance combine
   D) the company that owns the movie, television and serializa-
   tion rights to all of Ian Fleming's written work

6) TRUE or FALSE. James Bond was once a newspaper cartoon
   character.

12

7) Fleming married Lady Ann Rothermere in the old city of Port Maria, Jamaica. One of the songs played that day was later included in his book *THE MAN WITH THE GOLDEN GUN.* It is called
   A) "Angelina"
   B) "The Belly Lick"
   C) "Jump Up"
   D) "Underneath The Mango Tree"

8) TRUE or FALSE. The James Bond series was not a big seller in the United States until 1963, when President John F. Kennedy said that *GOLDFINGER* was one of his ten favorite books.

9) In 1958, Fleming said that he wanted _____ to play Agent 007 in the movies.
   A) Roger Moore
   B) David Niven
   C) Laurence Olivier
   D) James Stewart

10) How many James Bond stories did Fleming write?
   A) 13
   B) 14
   C) 18
   D) 21

2 THE NAME'S THE THING

11) For the women in his stories, Fleming created what has to be one of the most unusual collections of names ever assembled. Of the following, some are more famous (or infamous) than others. Can you match them to the correct story?

A)	Gala Brand	1)	*CASINO ROYALE*
B)	Tiffany Case	2)	*DIAMONDS ARE FOREVER*
C)	Pussy Galore	3)	*DOCTOR NO*
D)	Vesper Lynd	4)	*FROM A VIEW TO A KILL*
E)	Honeychile Rider	5)	*FROM RUSSIA WITH LOVE*
F)	Tatiana Romanova	6)	*GOLDFINGER*
G)	Mary Ann Russell	7)	*JAMES BOND IN NEW YORK*
H)	Solange	8)	*LIVE AND LET DIE*
I)	Simone Latrelle	9)	*MOONRAKER*
J)	Dominetta Vitale	10)	*THUNDERBALL*

12) TRUE or FALSE. Her father was disappointed she wasn't born a boy, so he gave her mother $1,000 and a compact from a famous store, before disappearing for good. That's how a character got the name "Tiffany Case."

13) James Bond frequently travels under the auspices of Universal Export, the cover name of the British Secret Service. But the building that houses this branch of British Intelligence also has a few other code names. Of the following, which isn't a name used on the building of Universal Export?
    A) Radio Tests, Ltd.
    B) Enquiries (Miss E. Twinning, O.B.E.)
    C) The Omnium Corporation
    D) F.I.R.C.O.

14) As the fictitious emissary from Universal Export, Bond himself has to use a variety of cover names. Sometimes he uses them while he masquerades as a businessman, sometimes not. Match the cover name with the appropriate Fleming story.

A)	David Barlow	1)	*CASINO ROYALE*
B)	Hilary Bray	2)	*DIAMONDS ARE FOREVER*
C)	John Bryce	3)	*DOCTOR NO*
D)	John Bryce (again!)	4)	*FROM RUSSIA WITH LOVE*
E)	Charles DaSilva	5)	*JAMES BOND IN NEW YORK*
F)	Peter Franks	6)	*LIVE AND LET DIE*
G)	Mark Hazard	7)	*ON HER MAJESTY'S SECRET SERVICE*
H)	David Somerset	8)	*THE MAN WITH THE GOLDEN GUN*
I)	Taro Todoroki	9)	*THE MAN WITH THE GOLDEN GUN*
J)	Frank Westmacott	10)	*YOU ONLY LIVE TWICE*

15) TRUE or FALSE. SPECTRE stands for "Special Executive For Terrorism, Revolution and Espionage."

3 THE MEN WHO CAME IN WITH THE GOLD

16) According to Bond producer Albert R. Broccoli, who gave him his start in the motion picture business?
    A) Charles K. Feldman, producer
    B) Howard Hughes, mega-billionaire
    C) Kevin McClory, producer
    D) Darryl F. Zanuck, producer

17) How did Albert R. Broccoli get the nickname "Cubby"?
    A) He looked like a cartoon character.
    B) He reminded all the cast and crew on *THE COCKLE-SHELL HEROES* of a bear cub.
    C) He was a big fan of the Chicago baseball team.
    D) It just evolved, based on the sounds of "C" and "B" in his last name.

18) On June 20, 1961, Broccoli and Harry Saltzman signed a deal with United Artists (under the auspices of Arthur Krim and David Picker) that launched the screen career of James Bond. Under that original deal, how many Bond pictures were called for?
    A) three pictures
    B) six pictures
    C) fourteen pictures
    D) as many Bond pictures as their company Eon Productions could make

19) TRUE or FALSE. Danjaq, the name of Eon Production's Swiss-based finance company, is a combination of the first names of the wives of Cubby Broccoli and Harry Saltzman.

20) What was Cubby Broccoli doing at the age of 24?
    A) working on his Uncle Pasquale's broccoli farm
    B) managing a movie house in Astoria, Queens
    C) running his cousin's casket company
    D) working for Howard Hawks within a week of emigrating to Los Angeles

21) What was the clinching evidence presented by producer Kevin McClory and his lawyers during the court case that ultimately gave him film and television rights to the Fleming property *THUNDERBALL*?
   A) a signed letter from Fleming dated years earlier
   B) McClory's hand-written notes containing material found in the final draft of the script
   C) privately taped recordings
   D) startling photographs of McClory himself

22) Eon Productions has produced only two other non-Bond films since it was formed in 1961. They were
   A) *CALL ME BWANA* and *CHITTY CHITTY BANG BANG*
   B) *THE IPCRESS FILE* and *FUNERAL IN BERLIN*
   C) *MAKE MINE MINK* and *BILLION DOLLAR BRAIN*
   D) *THAT MAN FROM RIO* and *THE BATTLE OF BRITAIN*

23) TRUE or FALSE. Cubby Broccoli once worked for Charles K. Feldman as a Hollywood agent. Feldman later produced the James Bond spoof, *CASINO ROYALE.*

24) What does Cubby mean when he refers to "bumps"?
   A) the beautiful chests of his female stars
   B) 007's rocky road to the screen
   C) the elements of each sequence that keep up the swift pace of the film
   D) He's never used the term.

25) Why did Broccoli and Saltzman hire Sean Connery to play James Bond, Agent 007, when other, bigger names were mentioned?
   A) Saltzman was impressed with the way Connery moved, and Broccoli thought he looked like "he had balls."
   B) Roger Moore was too busy shooting *THE ALASKANS.*
   C) Jimmy Stewart, Richard Burton and James Mason were all too expensive.
   D) They were personal friends of the Scottish actor and wanted to give him a break.

4 DOCTOR NO

26) The first time we see Sean Connery as Bond in *DOCTOR NO*
   A) he's lying in bed in the arms of a girl.
   B) he's running down a dark alley, being chased by agents of SPECTRE, desperately searching for his Aston Martin.
   C) he's playing *chemin de fer* at a London casino.
   D) he's playing *baccarat* at a Monte Carlo casino.

27) Every day at a certain time Strangways and his assistant call London by short-wave radio. When the film begins, Strangway's secretary is placing the daily radio message, and she introduces herself to London Station with the call letters
   A) W6N–G7W
   B) M7W–G6N
   C) G7N–W6W
   D) G3M–U7W

28) When 007 arrives in his Chelsea flat before going on assignment, he finds
   A) a naked woman in his bed.
   B) two naked women in his bed.
   C) a woman, wearing only a pajama top, playing golf.
   D) a woman, wearing only a bikini, playing golf.

29) What is the name of the girl in the arms of James Bond in the picture on the following page and who played her?
   A) Sylvia Trent, played by Dolores Keator
   B) Miss Taro, played by Zena Marshall
   C) Sylvia Trench, played by Eunice Gayson
   D) Mary, played by Eileen Warwick

30) TRUE or FALSE. This same character makes appearances in two other James Bond movies.

31) Who was responsible for putting a large, hairy spider in bed with 007? (see page 20)

18

James Bond at Home

(CREDIT: UPI)

A) Professor Dent
B) Honey Rider
C) Sister Rose
D) Miss Taro

32) Why is Bond sent to Jamaica?
   A) to placate a rather crotchety "M" who wants 007 out of his sight for a while
   B) to run a check on the missing Strangways and his secretary, who may have taken off with stolen Secret Service files and funds
   C) to get a little rest and relaxation
   D) to sort out the Strangways affair and check into whatever might be causing American rockets to go off course

33) According to the novel why is Bond forced to change weapons and turn in his faithful and trusty Beretta?

James Bond and a furry friend

(CREDIT: UPI)

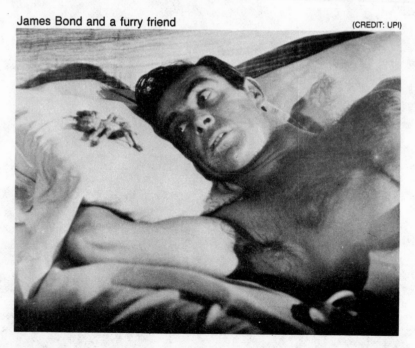

A) Everyone in the "double O" section is getting a new gun.

B) The silencer caught in his pocket during his last mission and he darn near got himself killed.

C) It is only a "lady's gun" and has hardly any stopping power.

D) "M" wants 007 to change guns—reason enough.

34) According to the novel, who is Doctor No and where did he come from?

A) He's a bird collector and land speculator from Haiti who made a killing selling the droppings of the Roseate Spoonbill.

B) He's the one man in a million whose heart is on the right side of his body from China.

C) He's an agent of SPECTRE, from Kobe, Japan.

D) He's a former Black Tong Society judo expert from Macao who lost his hands in a fight with a truck.

35) What is Doctor No's first name?

A) Ignacious

B) Horace

C) Julius

D) Junius

36) TRUE or FALSE. Quarrel (played by John Kitzmiller) is killed by a fire-breathing "Dragon" on the beaches of Jamaica.

37) When 007 begins making inquiries around the island, Professor Dent leaves for Crab Key and an emergency meeting with his boss. Unimpressed by the urgency of the visit, Doctor No instructs Dent to

A) stop bothering him about a stupid "policeman."

B) kill Bond.

C) return to Jamaica, and never set foot on Crab Key again.

D) read the *DOCTOR NO* novel and realize how lucky he is to be working, inasmuch as his character was created for the film and didn't exist in the book.

38) In the book, what does the factory on Crab Key do, besides serving as the cover for Doctor No's operation?
   A) mine for bauxite
   B) refine guano
   C) refine sugar
   D) refine coffee from the Blue Mountains

39) Ursula Andress appears as Honey Rider in *DOCTOR NO*. Producer Cubby Broccoli has said that she is still his favorite "Bond girl." Although she does not appear stark naked—as Fleming has her appear in the book—she ain't Shirley Temple, either. We learn from her brief narration in the movie that
   A) she used to stage wildlife shows in which one could watch a mongoose dance, a praying mantis eat its young and a scorpion with sunstroke sting itself to death.
   B) she was raped by her landlord, whom she soon killed by leaving a spider in his bed. It took a week for him to die.
   C) her parents were marine biologists who worked for Doctor No.
   D) her father was killed by Doctor No, as is written in the book.

40) In the movie, when Bond first sees Honey rising out of the sea like Botticelli's *Venus,* she's
   A) wearing nothing but a bikini and hunting knife, singing "Underneath The Mango Tree."
   B) wearing nothing at all, singing "Marion."

URSULA ANDRESS as Honeychile Rider

(COURTESY OF ARTIST)

C) wearing a Chinese kimono and looking for seashells.

D) fixing her canoe on the beach.

41) In the book, what is "wrong" with Honeychile Rider?
A) She is barren.
B) She kills everyone who ever loves her with poisonous animals.
C) She has a broken nose.
D) She is unable to wear shoes.

42) Who lives at 2171 Magenta Drive?
A) Professor Dent
B) Pleydell-Smith
C) Commander Strangways
D) Miss Taro

43) We first see the black steel hands of Doctor No when
A) he goes to shake hands with Commander Bond.
B) Bond tries to shake his hand, before dinner.
C) he pulls back the bed sheets covering a sleeping 007.
D) he's unable to grasp the steel supports of a catwalk, falling helplessly into the atomic reactor.

44) After Bond successfully defeats Doctor No, he races through the crumbling complex to find Honey
A) wearing nothing but her bikini, smoking cigarettes with her guards.
B) lying on a concrete floor wearing only the top half of her Chinese costume.
C) tied to the floor in her bikini, surrounded by crabs.
D) racing through the complex, machine gun in hand, shouting "James!"

45) Identify the stolen painting in Doctor No's fancy living room.
A) Rembrandt's *Mona Lisa*
B) Goya's portrait of Wellington
C) Van Gogh's last self-portrait
D) Whistler's *Mother*

5 BE CAREFUL WITH THAT THING, WILL YA?

(CREDIT: INTERARMS, Alexandria, VA)

A Walther PPK

46) Pictured above is Agent 007's favorite gun, his Walther PPK. Used in most of his cinematic adventures, what gun did it replace?
   A) .25 Beretta
   B) .28 Beretta
   C) .38 Smith and Wesson
   D) .45 Colt

47) And where is this nasty little weapon generally kept?
   A) in a Burns-Mantle shoulder holster under Bond's left shoulder
   B) in a Berns-Martin shoulder holster under Bond's left shoulder
   C) in 007's attaché case
   D) under the dashboard of whatever car he's using

48) In the novel *THE MAN WITH THE GOLDEN GUN*, Scaramanga's famous Golden Gun is made from
   A) pens and a cigarette lighter.
   B) the tops of cologne bottles and the handle of a man's razor.
   C) a solid gold, prefabricated .45 Colt revolver.
   D) sugar and spice and everything nice.

49) In how many films does 007 crack open a safe with some sort of electronic device?

A) 3
B) 4
C) 7
D) all of them

50) Bond's famous attaché case in *FROM RUSSIA WITH LOVE* is really the first example of gadgetry gone wild in the 007 films. This briefcase contains
   A) a folding rifle, concealed throwing knife, gold sovereigns and an exploding talcum powder canister.
   B) 20 rounds of ammunition, a flat throwing knife, a folding rifle, an antiaircraft bazooka and 50 gold sovereigns.
   C) ammunition, a knife, a gun, a geiger counter and gold coins.
   D) ammunition, a folding rifle, a flat throwing knife, gold sovereigns and a tear-gas canister.

51) In what film does Bond use his wristwatch to cut himself free of a rope?
   A) *YOU ONLY LIVE TWICE*
   B) *LIVE AND LET DIE*
   C) *THE SPY WHO LOVED ME*
   D) *OCTOPUSSY*

52) Which film features "Q" describing the properties of radioactive lint?
   A) *YOU ONLY LIVE TWICE*
   B) *ON HER MAJESTY'S SECRET SERVICE*
   C) *DIAMONDS ARE FOREVER*
   D) He never describes this tool.

53) In the novel *GOLDFINGER,* the DB III that James Bond drives is equipped with all sorts of gadgets, except
   A) a homing device.
   B) a long-barreled Colt .45.
   C) front and rear lights that change color.
   D) rotating license plates.

54) This one seems simple enough: Match the weapon or gadget to the film in which it is first used (only one gadget per film, so think carefully).

A) geiger counter   1) *DIAMONDS ARE FOREVER*

B) fake fingerprints   2) *DOCTOR NO*

C) rocket-firing cigarette   3) *NEVER SAY NEVER AGAIN*

D) jet-pack   4) *THE SPY WHO LOVED ME*

E) exploding pen   5) *THUNDERBALL*

F) ski-pole with gun inside   6) *YOU ONLY LIVE TWICE*

55) James Bond has never been known for making a dull entrance. In fact, in two films he appears underwater, wearing a fake animal on his head. Name the films and the animals.

A) *THUNDERBALL* and a seagull, *OCTOPUSSY* and an alligator

B) *GOLDFINGER* and a seagull, *OCTOPUSSY* and an alligator

C) *THE SPY WHO LOVED ME* and a shark, *FOR YOUR EYES ONLY* and a seagull

D) *NEVER SAY NEVER AGAIN* and a shark, *CASINO ROYALE* and a walrus

6 FROM RUSSIA WITH LOVE

56) In the opening sequence, Donovan Grant stalks a James Bond "double" through the bushes and eventually chokes him to death. How long does it take?
   A) one minute, thirty seconds
   B) one minute, fifty-two seconds
   C) thirty seconds
   D) two minutes, twenty-five seconds

57) When we first meet Kronsteen, he's playing chess at the Grand Master's Tournament in Venice. As the game draws to a climax, he receives a mysterious message demanding his immediate presence elsewhere. What move does he make to end the game quickly?
   A) Queen takes Rook; puts Macadams in check.
   B) Knight takes Bishop; puts Macadams in check.
   C) King to Rook 2; Macadams concedes defeat.
   D) Queen to King 4; Macadams concedes defeat.

58) TRUE or FALSE. As in the novel, when we first meet "Number One" (who we'll soon learn is Blofeld), he's stroking a white cat.

59) Ian Fleming is pictured on the next page with the actress who played Tatiana Romanova in *FROM RUSSIA WITH LOVE*. In real life
   A) she was runner-up in the 1960 Miss Universe pagent.
   B) she could speak seven languages—but not English.
   C) she was runner-up in the 1960 Miss World pageant.
   D) she was a political refugee from a Warsaw-pact country.

60) Tatiana is called to a private meeting with Rosa Klebb. She is given the once-over, and her mission is explained. According to Klebb, what will happen to Tatiana if she refuses to go along with the plan?
   A) She will be shot.
   B) She will not leave the room alive.
   C) She will be sent to Siberia.
   D) She will be boiled and stuffed.

IAN FLEMING with actress who played Tahana Romanova in From Russia With Love (CREDIT: UPI)

61) It's been a long, hot and eventful day for 007 by the time he returns to his hotel for the evening. Once there he finds yet another distraction—the lovely Tatiana lying naked in his bed. Small talk gives way to even smaller talk, and soon they're in bed together. Tatiana fears something will be too big. What?
   A) Well, you know. . . .
   B) her mouth
   C) her eyes
   D) the bed

62) In the novel *FROM RUSSIA WITH LOVE,* we learn some details about May, 007's Scottish housekeeper. She is responsible for taking care of his flat and keeping his refrigerator filled with food, but she
   A) never gives in to any of Bond's sexual advances.
   B) never makes his bed, insisting that, considering what went on in there he should make it himself.
   C) never calls him "sir" (she goes only as far as to call him "s——").
   D) never asks for a raise.

63) Who is known as "the Wizard of Ice"?
   A) General Grubozaboyschikov
   B) Kronsteen
   C) Rosa Klebb
   D) Donovan Grant

64) Rosa Klebb hits Donovan Grant _____ and finds him suitably fit for duty.
   A) in the groin with her foot
   B) in the stomach with brass knuckles
   C) in the face with a rake
   D) on the head with a brick

65) Kerim Bey takes Bond to visit the gypsy camp, pictured on the next page. Since the two girls shown are in love with the same man, they must fight each other to the death (a quaint gypsy custom). What are the names of the two female characters?

29

(CREDIT: UPI)

A) Zora and Nadja
B) Aliza and Vida
C) Leila and Ziza
D) Vida and Zora

66) Just before one of the girls smashes a bottle over the head of the other, a fight breaks out between the gypsies and the Bulgars in which Bond is almost killed by a man brandishing a sabre. How does Bond live to tell the tale?
A) The man trips and falls on his own sabre.
B) Donovan Grant watches 007 throughout the fight and shoots the sabre-rattler in the nick of time.
C) Kerim Bey kills the man with the sabre, and Vavra is the unlucky recipient of another bullet meant for Commander Bond.
D) 007, hero of the British Secret Service, runs away when no one is looking.

67) The Bulgarian killer Krilencu is killed by Kerim Bey as he escapes through the mouth of Anita Ekberg, whose face adorns a film advertisement on the side of a building. In the novel, the female on the wall is Marilyn Monroe. Why was this changed in the movie?
A) Miss Monroe had recently died.
B) Broccoli and Saltzman were big Anita Ekberg fans and wanted to give her some free publicity.
C) Miss Ekberg was married to art director Syd Cain.
D) It was easier and less expensive to use the poster because it was already painted on the wall the producers had chosen.

68) In his office, Kerim Bey is quietly contemplating the troubles of the world while his girl friend, lying on the settee, chews her beads and whines for attention. Finally addressing the situation, he stands up and says,
A) "Here we go again."
B) "You want to give an old man a stroke."
C) "Back to the salt mines."
D) "I have too many sons already. . . ."

69) Before becoming head of Station "T" (Turkey) for the British Secret Service, Kerim Bey used to
   A) break chains and bend steel with his teeth.
   B) promote gun smuggling to anyone who'd pay him.
   C) sell rugs in a Turkish bazaar.
   D) work as a mind reader in a circus.

70) While riding aboard the Orient Express, Grant does something that later gives Bond a clue to his true identity. What does he do?
   A) He slips 007 a sleeping pill.
   B) He orders red wine with fish.
   C) He says he knows Zagreb very well, a moment after he has said he's never been there.
   D) He orders red caviar instead of black, and asks for his Stolichnaya "on the rocks."

71) What does Tatiana give Bond inside the famous St. Sophia mosque (pictured on the next page)?
   A) the French disease
   B) the Lektor
   C) the plans of the Soviet Embassy
   D) a description of the Lektor

72) Why does "M" ask Miss Moneypenny to leave the room while he and others listen to a taped conversation between Bond and Miss Romanova?
   A) He's a sexist sailor who considers Moneypenny a worthless female.
   B) The tape contains highly classified information, and she's not properly cleared to listen to it.
   C) He's afraid she'll get jealous hearing the intimate details of 007's sex life.
   D) Bond is about to recount a tale concerning "M" and himself carousing in Japan.

73) Although in the movie 007 kills Grant with his own deadly wristwatch, this differs greatly from the way he kills the man in the book. How does Grant leave this world in the book?

32

Interior of the St. Sophia Mosque

(CREDIT: TURKISH OFFICE OF TOURISM)

A) He's tossed out of the window as the train passes over the Danube.

B) He's electrocuted aboard the train by a broken light socket and a piece of wire.

C) He's stabbed in the crotch by Bond, who then shoots him with a deadly copy of *War And Peace*.

D) His face is tied to a lavatory seat, and 007 flushes him to death.

74) What is the name of the poison in Rosa Klebb's shoes?
   A) curare
   B) strychnine
   C) fugu
   D) tropical swill

75) TRUE or FALSE. At the end of the film, as he rides through the canals of Venice with Tatiana, Bond is about to throw away the compromising film footage of himself and Miss Romanova, when common sense (and a dash of prurient interest) prompts him to keep the footage for further study.

7 HE WENT THATAWAY

76) In what film(s) does the famous Aston Martin DB V make an appearance?
   A) *GOLDFINGER, THUNDERBALL, ON HER MAJESTY'S SECRET SERVICE* and *DIAMONDS ARE FOREVER*
   B) *GOLDFINGER* and *THUNDERBALL*
   C) *GOLDFINGER, THUNDERBALL* and *DIAMONDS ARE FOREVER*
   D) *GOLDFINGER* only

77) When does Bond use the famous ejector seat in his Aston Martin?
   A) at "Q" branch during a test run of the car
   B) while Oddjob sits next to him on the ride to Auric enterprises
   C) in the opening sequence of *THUNDERBALL*
   D) during the return ride to Goldfinger's Swiss factory, and the victim is an unsuspecting guard

78) Where is the control for the ejector seat?
   A) on the steering wheel
   B) in the gearshift handle
   C) on the floor near the gas pedal
   D) in the console between the front seats

79) What countries are represented on the revolving license plates?
   A) England, France and Germany
   B) England, Germany and Sweden
   C) England, France and Italy
   D) England, France and Switzerland

80) TRUE or FALSE. Bond uses the rear-end "water squirter" only in *THUNDERBALL* (see photograph on the bottom of page 37).

BMT 216 A

Sᴇᴀɴ Cᴏɴɴᴇʀʏ with his Aston Martin

(CREDIT: ASTON MARTIN)

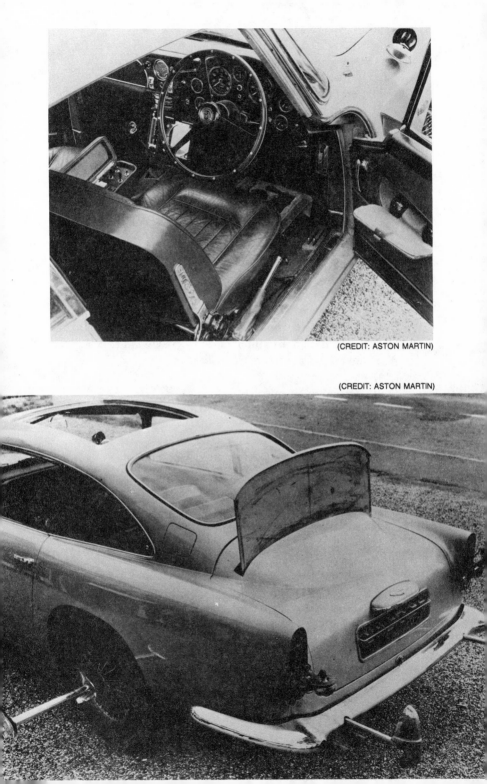

(CREDIT: ASTON MARTIN)

(CREDIT: ASTON MARTIN)

81) What do the "offside lamp clusters" do?
   A) eject specially designed nails
   B) shoot out oil in order to cause an oil slick
   C) generate smoke in order to make a smoke screen
   D) expose two Browning machine guns

82) In what film does Bond arrive at the villain's hideout in a hot-air balloon?
   A) *CASINO ROYALE*
   B) *YOU ONLY LIVE TWICE*
   C) *FOR YOUR EYES ONLY*
   D) *OCTOPUSSY*

83) Using the Lotus Esprit pictured on the top of page 39, Bond and Anya outmaneuver one of Stromberg's henchmen in *THE SPY WHO LOVED ME*. But after driving off a dock and into the Mediterranean, they are still pursued by Naomi in her helicopter. What does Bond use to get rid of her?
   A) his charm
   B) ground-to-air missiles
   C) aerial land mines
   D) smoke-bomb rockets

84) The Lotus Esprit in *THE SPY WHO LOVED ME*
   A) was manufactured by Lotus as a fully operational sub for use in the film.
   B) is delivered personally by "Q" to Bond in South America.
   C) comes in six different shells and really works underwater.
   D) reappears only once again, in *FOR YOUR EYES ONLY*.

85) This toy car (see page 39, bottom), manufactured by Corgi, is a scale replica of a car 007 is forced to drive in a chase in which of the following films?
   A) *FROM RUSSIA WITH LOVE*
   B) *THE MAN WITH THE GOLDEN GUN*
   C) *MOONRAKER*
   D) *FOR YOUR EYES ONLY*

Lotus Esprit underwater

(CREDIT: DON GRIFFIN, PERRY SUBMARINES)

86) What happens to the car?
   A) It ends up in a pool.
   B) It ends up in a tree.
   C) It ends up in a pile of cement powder.
   D) It gets turned upside down with 007 inside.

87) What kind of car does Bond drive in *DIAMONDS ARE FOREVER*?
   A) an Aston Martin
   B) a Datsun
   C) a Mustang
   D) a Toyota

Citroen deux chevaux, Corgi Toy Car

(CREDIT: REEVES INTERNATIONAL)

88) James Bond enjoys traveling by train. In the written works of Ian Fleming, he takes five train rides. Match the train with the story it appears in.

A) The Laguna Express (Rome to Venice)

B) The Orient Express (Istanbul to Paris)

C) The Silver Meteor (Miami to New York City)

D) The Silver Phantom (New York City to St. Petersburg)

E) The 20th Century (New York City to Chicago)

1) *DIAMONDS ARE FOREVER*

2) *FROM RUSSIA WITH LOVE*

3) *GOLDFINGER*

4) *LIVE AND LET DIE*

5) *RISICO*

89) In how many films does James Bond have a fight scene aboard a moving train?
   A) one
   B) two
   C) four
   D) five

90) In what film does the "Wetbike" put in an appearance?
   A) *THUNDERBALL*
   B) *THE SPY WHO LOVED ME*
   C) *FOR YOUR EYES ONLY*
   D) *NEVER SAY NEVER AGAIN*

91) In the pre-title sequence, 007 is somewhere in Latin America and in the arms of a beautiful girl named Bonita. As he kisses her, another man enters the room. How does Bond know someone else has arrived?
    A) He feels the butt of a gun against his skull.
    B) He sees the man's reflection in a highly polished cigarette case.
    C) He sees the man's reflection in the girl's pupil.
    D) He sees the man reflected in the tiny mirror device attached to his Rollex Oyster Perpetual.

92) Also in the pre-title sequence, we see Bond destroy the drug refinery of a big-time heroin smuggler. How was the drug being smuggled out?
    A) in fish tanks
    B) in ice cream
    C) in bananas
    D) in sugar tins

93) While sunning at the Fountainbleu Hotel in Miami Beach, Bond is given a massage and rubdown by a girl named Dink. Who played Dink?
    A) Nadja Regin
    B) Margaret Nolan
    C) Stephanie Powers
    D) Maggie Lacey

94) Also at the Fountainbleu is Auric Goldfinger. We get our first glimpse of him at poolside, where he's red as a lobster and playing cards with a man named
    A) Brunskill.
    B) Du Pont.
    C) Simmons.
    D) Willis.

95) TRUE or FALSE. In the novel *GOLDFINGER*, we learn that Bond loves Britain's ubiquitous cup of tea, and that he plans to write a book on self-defense entitled *Stay Alive!*

96) After having made love to Jill Masterson, why does Bond get up, leaving her alone and wearing nothing more than his pajama top?
   A) She's a wild minx and he needs a breath of air.
   B) She's thirsty and he's going to fetch a cooler bottle of champagne.
   C) She's been painted gold while they slept together, and he's a bit sickened by that fact.
   D) She's asked him to turn around while she readies a surprise (something cut out of the final print).

97) Who plays Jill Masterson, the girl painted gold?
   A) Shirley Eaton
   B) Honor Blackman
   C) Tilly Soames
   D) Tania Mallet

98) Why does Goldfinger have Jill painted gold in the movie?
   A) He enjoys the sensation of "making love" to gold; unfortunately, by painting her entire body, he kills her.
   B) She doesn't ask permission to sleep with 007.
   C) It is Oddjob who paints her gold, and he subsequently kills her with his metal-rimmed hat.
   D) He wants to present a life-sized Oscar at the 1965 Academy Awards.

99) Bond's tardiness reporting to a meeting in "M" 's office incurs the wrath of his old boss, who then threatens to replace 007 with
   A) a trained cocker spaniel.
   B) Agent 008.
   C) Agent 009.
   D) the chief duty officer.

100) Who plays the character Oddjob?
   A) Wo Fat
   B) Sax Rohmer

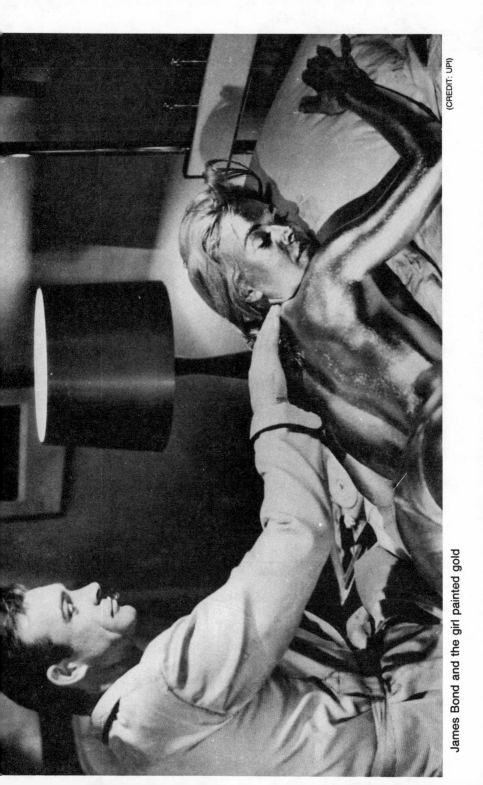

James Bond and the girl painted gold

(CREDIT: UPI)

C) Harold Sakata
D) Burt Kwok

101) Why can't Oddjob speak?
A) No one ever asks him.
B) He never learned how.
C) His vocal chords were severed when he was a small child.
D) He has a cleft palate.

102) Oddjob's nationality is
A) Chinese
B) Korean
C) Japanese
D) Mongolian

103) In the movie *GOLDFINGER,* what kind of golf ball does Goldfinger use, and how does Bond foil his effort to cheat?
A) Dunlop 65, #1; Bond has the caddie switch balls.
B) Dunlop 65, #7; Bond has the caddie switch balls.
C) Slazenger #1; Bond switches the ball himself at hole 17.
D) Slazenger #7; Bond switches the ball himself at hole 17.

104) After Goldfinger loses the game of golf, Oddjob does something only Oddjob could do. What?
A) He crushes 007's foot with the Nazi gold bar.
B) He tosses his hat and slices the head off a stone statue.
C) He tosses his hat and slices the head off the caddy.
D) He crushes a golf-club mallet with his bare hands.

105) _____ is the name given to Goldfinger's planned attack on Fort Knox.
A) Operation All The Way
B) Operation Home Run
C) Operation Grand Slam
D) Operation Out Of The Park

106) In the movie, Goldfinger tries to slice Bond with a laser beam. In the novel, he

SEAN CONNERY with GERT FROBE as Goldfinger

(CREDIT: UPI)

A) uses a laser beam, too.
B) uses a log-splitting buzz saw.
C) uses a barrel of molten gold.
D) is gassed along with the gangsters.

107) Upon leaving Europe for the United States, Bond is drugged and taken aboard Goldfinger's private jet. When he awakens
A) he's greeted by a woman claiming to be Pussy Galore.
B) he fights with Oddjob.
C) he's greeted with a martini and finger sandwiches.
D) he uses his concealed knife to cut himself loose.

108) In the film version of *GOLDFINGER*, 007 has a fight to the death with Oddjob inside Fort Knox. But how is Oddjob killed in the book?
A) He's killed in the same painfully shocking way as in the film.
B) He's caught in Goldfinger's Swiss smelting plant.
C) He's sucked out a broken perspex window aboard a plane after a nervous James Bond shoots a hole through it.
D) He's killed by Felix Leiter at Fort Knox.

109) The name of the nerve gas Goldfinger is about to release on the 41,000 troops stationed around Fort Knox is
A) Ice Nine
B) Zyclon B
C) Delta 9
D) Dilithium crystals

110) When does Bond use the front machine gun on his Aston Martin?
A) when he shoots the old lady at the guardhouse
B) when he tries to flatten Tilly's tires
C) when he breaks through the railing at the customs house
D) when he shoots at his own reflection

46

(CREDIT: ASTON MARTIN)

9 SURE IT LOOKS EASY

111) What film features a spectacular 110-foot leap through the air by a motorboat?
   A) *THUNDERBALL*
   B) *LIVE AND LET DIE*
   C) *THE MAN WITH THE GOLDEN GUN*
   D) *MOONRAKER*

112) In what films do men or women fall to their deaths from airborne planes or helicopters?
   A) *GOLDFINGER, MOONRAKER, OCTOPUSSY*
   B) *GOLDFINGER, YOU ONLY LIVE TWICE, MOON-RAKER, FOR YOUR EYES ONLY, OCTOPUSSY*
   C) *GOLDFINGER, THE MAN WITH THE GOLDEN GUN, MOONRAKER*
   D) *GOLDFINGER, THUNDERBALL, LIVE AND LET DIE, MOONRAKER, OCTOPUSSY*

113) What kind of car is used to perform the 360-degree aerial spin in *THE MAN WITH THE GOLDEN GUN*?
   A) AMC Hornet
   B) AMC Javelin
   C) AMC Matador
   D) AMC Maverick

114) TRUE or FALSE. The opening ski jump in *THE SPY WHO LOVED ME* was shot on location in Austria, and is based on a photographic advertisement for Courvoisier.

115) In what film do we see 007 ski with only one ski?
   A) none
   B) *ON HER MAJESTY'S SECRET SERVICE*
   C) *THE SPY WHO LOVED ME*
   D) *FOR YOUR EYES ONLY*

116) In which film does a fight break out inside a ritzy casino?
   A) *THUNDERBALL*
   B) *CASINO ROYALE*
   C) *ON HER MAJESTY'S SECRET SERVICE*
   D) *THE MAN WITH THE GOLDEN GUN*

117) In order to shoot the sumo wrestler's sequence in *YOU ONLY LIVE TWICE,* _____ sumo wrestlers were placed on call for 3 days in Tokyo.
   A) 12
   B) 50
   C) 100
   D) more than a thousand

118) TRUE or FALSE. In *LIVE AND LET DIE,* a London Transport double-decker bus is painted to look like those on the island of San Monique. Although Roger Moore does most of the actual driving of the bus—with a brave Jane Seymour strapped down in the back—neither performer is actually on the bus when the top level is sliced off.

119) While not as physically dangerous as falling from 1,000 feet without a parachute, playing cards or betting on other games has landed 007 in pretty difficult situations. Ian Fleming was an avid gamesman himself, and much of his best writing can be found in passages concerning game playing. Match the game or sport to the story it appears in.

   A) *baccarat*   1) *CASINO ROYALE*
   B) bobsledding   2) *DIAMONDS ARE FOREVER*
   C) bridge   3) *FROM RUSSIA WITH LOVE*
   D) *chemin de fer*   4) *GOLDFINGER*
   E) chess   5) *THE HILDEBRAND RARITY*
   F) fishing   6) *LIVE AND LET DIE*
   G) fortunetelling   7) *MOONRAKER*

49

H) golf
I) horse racing
J) scissors-cut-paper

8) *ON HER MAJESTY'S SECRET SERVICE*
9) *THUNDERBALL*
10) *YOU ONLY LIVE TWICE*

120) James Bond has fought villains in a variety of settings, from outer space to between the sheets. But in which film and in which city does he fight a man in an elevator?
   A) *THUNDERBALL,* in Nassau
   B) *CASINO ROYALE,* in Monte Carlo
   C) *DIAMONDS ARE FOREVER,* in Amsterdam
   D) *THE SPY WHO LOVED ME,* at sea

121) TRUE or FALSE. *THUNDERBALL* opens with James Bond attending a funeral in France for one Colonel Boivard. At the home of Boivard's widow, 007 offers his condolences by punching the "deceased" in the face.

122) Who plays the character Count Lippe?
A) Frank Cousins
B) Guy Williams
C) Guy Doleman
D) DeForest Kelly

123) After a brush with death on the motorized stretching machine, 007 makes his nurse feel pretty guilty. As he successfully seduces Patricia, they both disappear into
A) his bed.
B) the steam room.
C) the irrigation room.
D) the drilling room.

124) Lucianna Paluzzi plays the beautiful and deadly agent of SPEC-TRE named Fiona (see next page). Who does she kill with the rockets of her motorcycle?
A) Paula Caplan
B) Major Derval
C) Count Lippe
D) Bob Simmons

125) Bond first meets Fiona along the roadside as he thumbs for a ride. Later, when she decides it's time to have Commander Bond killed, Fiona sneaks into 007's room and takes a bath. When he arrives, James is pleasantly surprised to see her in his tub and hands her _____ so she can get dressed.
A) nothing
B) a washcloth

LUCIANNA PALUZZI on her motorcycle

(CREDIT: ROBERT FRESON/ESQUIRE ASSOCIATES c.1965)

C) a towel
D) her slippers

126) What is the symbol on the ring worn by SPECTRE agents?
   A) a red square with a black spike through it
   B) a black circle with a "crooked sickle" cutting through it
   C) an octopus with a skull as its head
   D) a pair of lightning bolts

127) Before setting out for Nassau, Bond is given a clue to Domino's whereabouts. What is it?

- A) a beauty mark on her face
- B) two moles on her left thigh
- C) a tiny scar on her lower back
- D) an ankle bracelet with her name on it

128) Pictured above is Emilio Largo, Agent #2 in SPECTRE. What is the name of the actor who plays him?
- A) Rudolpho Cellini
- B) Adolfo Celi
- C) Adolphe Menjou
- D) Paul Stassino

129) When we first see Largo, he's entering a building that we will soon learn is the headquarters for SPECTRE. Where is SPECTRE's home office located?
- A) Boulevard Haussman, Paris
- B) Park Lane, London
- C) Kurfurstendamm, Berlin
- D) Lindwurmstrasse, Munich

130) Although Fleming gave it a different cover name in the novel *THUNDERBALL,* what is the name inscribed outside the movie's European office of SPECTRE when Largo first arrives?
- A) International Brotherhood for the Assistance of Stateless Persons

B) Transcontinental Union for Refugees and Victims of War Torn Territories

C) International Brotherhood for the Resistance of Oppression

D) International Alliance of Oppressed Peoples

131) In the novel, we meet the board of directors of SPECTRE for the first time. Fleming describes how it was first organized by Ernst Stavro Blofeld, and how its members were chosen. Among "the 20" were 2 scientists, 3 Sicilians from the Mafia, 3 Corsicans from the Union Corse, 3 former members of SMERSH, 3 former members of Tito's Yugoslav Secret Police, 3 Highland Turks, and

A) 3 former members of the Red Lightning Tongs.

B) 3 former members of the Corleone Mafia family.

C) 3 former agents of the *Sonderdienst.*

D) 3 former members of varying small-time crime outfits, unknown to all except those with a "need to know."

132) Ernst Stavro Blofeld, born on May 28, 1908, is

A) Dutch.

B) German.

C) Polish.

D) Swiss.

133) Claudine Auger plays the character Domino in *THUNDER-BALL.* According to Fleming, what did Domino do before she met Largo?

A) She was a high-class hooker.

B) She was a dancer with Les Folies Bergeres.

C) She was studying to be a bartender.

D) She was an actress with a strange interest in cigarettes.

134) James Bond gives Domino a geiger counter, which she brings aboard Largo's yacht. When he realizes what she's doing, how does Largo plan to torture her?

A) by beating her with the tail of a sting ray

B) with ice cubes and a lit cigar

CLAUDINE AUGER

(CREDIT: ROBERT FRESON/ESQUIRE ASSOCIATES © 1965)

C) with soft cushions and a comfy chair

D) with tropical insects and a surgical knife

135) How does the climax of *THUNDERBALL* the novel differ from that of *THUNDERBALL* the movie?

    A) In the movie, Bond kills Largo aboard the main deck of the *Disco Volante.*

    B) In the movie, Domino kills Largo aboard the main deck of the *Disco Volante.*

    C) In the movie, Domino harpoons Largo underwater with a CO_2 harpoon gun, instead of with her Luger pistol.

    D) In the movie, Domino avenges her torture by tying Largo to the rear rudder of a hovercraft, then racing it along the coral reef.

136) What happens to the man who hides in the shower of Bond's hotel room?

    A) He is thoroughly embarrassed when a nude 007 jumps in for a shower.

    B) He overhears Bond discussing plans with Felix Leiter, and quietly makes his exit.

    C) He is drenched with water and fed to the sharks for failing.

    D) He is shot dead by Bond with a CO_2 harpoon gun.

137) _____ and _____ are the names of two of Largo's henchmen.

    A) Vargas and Kenniston

    B) Vargas and Quist

    C) Piner and Caplan

    D) Boren and Cousins

138) TRUE or FALSE. The *Disco Volante* is a sailing vessel registered in Liberia.

139) In the film as in the novel, SPECTRE's plan calls for the hijacking and theft of two atomic bombs. What is the ransom demanded from the NATO powers?

A) 100 million pounds worth of uncut diamonds
B) 100 million pounds worth of gold bullion
C) 100 million pounds worth of unmarked bills
D) 200 million pounds worth of gold, and a pardon for all past crimes committed by agents of SPECTRE

140) How does the movie *THUNDERBALL* end?
A) Bond and Domino are in the hospital, sharing the same bed, when Felix Leiter stumbles in with a medal from the United Nations.
B) Bond and Domino are left floating at sea in a large yellow raft, as 007 continues to look for sea-urchin spines on various parts of her body.
C) Bond and Domino are scooped up by a passing plane and winched into the skies.
D) Bond and Domino fall into the sea, making love amidst the coral—causing quite a disturbance among the local fish population.

11 FIRST WE BLOW UP THE EARTH

141) A more bizarre collection of criminals and scoundrels never existed. Not only are the schemes of Fleming's villains fantastic,
their appearance is often just as strange. Below are descriptions
of people only their mothers could love. Match the deformities
with the people they belong to.

A) a head the size of a football, no eyelashes or eyebrows, golden irises sur-
rounding black pupils

B) tight red hair parted in
the middle, ears that
don't match, one blood-
shot eye that is larger
than the other

C) moonshaped-face, fat
body, five feet tall

D) polished skull, Da-
liesque eyebrows, steel
pincers for hands, metal
eyeballs

E) Humphrey Bogart lisp,
hard and fat body

F) bland high forehead,
gray-black moustache,
mane of white hair

G) hunchback with bright
red hair

H) long hair, 168 pounds,
ears that stick out and
dark green contact
lenses

I) a toadlike figure, thick
legs and pear-shaped
hips

1) Mr. Big

2) Blofeld in *THUNDER-
BALL*

3) Blofeld in *ON HER
MAJESTY'S SECRET
SERVICE*

4) Blofeld in *YOU ONLY
LIVE TWICE*

5) Hugo "Hugger" Drax

6) Auric Goldfinger

7) Rosa Klebb

8) Milton Krest

9) Le Chiffre

J) black eyes surrounded entirely by whites, 280 pounds, long and pointy hands, black crew cut

10) Doctor No

K) very dark brown eyes with whites showing around the entire iris, small feet, feminine mouth

11) Shady Tree

142) What was "Red" Grant's first name?
   A) Boris
   B) Donovan
   C) Frank
   D) Kurt

143) Who plays Rosa Klebb?
   A) the wife of Bertolt Brecht
   B) the wife of Moss Hart
   C) the wife of Ronald Reagan
   D) the wife of Kurt Weill

144) In what film do we first see Blofeld's face?
   A) *DOCTOR NO*
   B) *FROM RUSSIA WITH LOVE*
   C) *THUNDERBALL*
   D) *YOU ONLY LIVE TWICE*

145) TRUE or FALSE. Fatima Blush is a character created specifically for *NEVER SAY NEVER AGAIN*.

146) Although we already know the name of the actor who played Oddjob (see question 100), the credits of *GOLDFINGER* list yet another name for this physically imposing actor. What is it?
   A) Tish Tosh
   B) Tosh Togo
   C) Tosh Chang
   D) Chang Kisch

147) Who provides the hands that stroke the cat during the early appearances of "Number One"?
   A) Eric Pohlman
   B) George Baker
   C) Anthony Dawson
   D) Donald Pleasance

148) Stromberg doesn't believe in shaking hands because
   A) like Howard Hughes, he's bacteriophobic.
   B) he has webbing between his fingers.
   C) the touch of human skin disgusts him; he's more comfortable touching fish.
   D) he has a phobia about losing his hand.

149) In the movie *CASINO ROYALE,* how does Le Chiffre meet his end?
   A) He's at the casino when it explodes.
   B) He's electrocuted, along with Evelyn Tremble.
   C) Vesper Lynd shoots him with her bagpipes.
   D) A SMERSH agent shoots him through a television screen.

150) How many actors have contributed, in whole or in part, to playing Ernst Stavro Blofeld on the screen?
   A) 3
   B) 4
   C) 7
   D) 10

151) Since *CASINO ROYALE* was Ian Fleming's first novel, at the time of its publication he had no following in the United States. Although the book had sold moderately well in Great Britain, the American publishers feared that its title might not help sales (Americans being unsure about the correct pronunciation of the word "Royale"). What was the title of the book when it was first published in the United States?
   A) *THE NATURE OF EVIL*
   B) *THE CRAWLING OF THE SKIN*
   C) *TOO HOT TO HANDLE*
   D) *CASINO ROYALE*

152) TRUE or FALSE. James Bond smokes up to 70 cigarettes a day by the time *CASINO ROYALE* takes place. His cigarettes are a special blend of Balkan and Turkish tobaccos made exclusively for him by Morland's of Grosvenor Street, and he keeps 50 of them in his gun-metal cigarette case at all times. Each cigarette has two gold bands around the filter.

153) In the book, we learn very little about 007 and his past. What we do learn is how he got his "double O" license-to-kill number. How did he get it?
   A) by winning a crap game
   B) by displaying enormous ability and intelligence through-out his period of ordinary fieldwork, and by demonstrat-ing considerable skill on the firing range
   C) for supervising the Allied evacuation from France during World War II, as Fleming himself had done
   D) by murdering a Japanese cipher expert in Rockefeller Center, and a Norwegian spy with a knife

154) In this scene from *CASINO ROYALE* (see next page), David Niven as Sir James Bond sits down to a meal in Scotland. Which actress is his hostess, and what is the name of her character?

(COURTESY: COLUMBIA PICTURES)

A) Dana Wynter as Agent Mimi
B) Deborah Kerr as Agent Mimi
C) Susannah York as Mata Hari
D) Vanessa Redgrave as Vesper Lynd

155) Why is Bond sent to this Scottish castle in the first place?
   A) to enjoy a good haggis before heading off to fight SMERSH
   B) to inform the lady that "M" has been killed and to return his red toupee
   C) to play a game of "concrete" medicine ball with some Scottish Lords
   D) to hunt for grouse in the Highlands

156) When the film opens, Sir James Bond is retired from the spy business, passing his time
   A) reading books and growing flowers.
   B) experimenting with drugs and little girls.
   C) raising lions and playing Debussy.
   D) collecting stamps and World War II bombshell casings.

157) Although David Niven plays James Bond in *CASINO ROYALE*, who plays 007?
   A) Woody Allen
   B) Terence Cooper
   C) Ronnie Corbett
   D) Derek Nimmo

158) What does Evelyn Tremble (played by Peter Sellers) do every time someone calls him "James Bond"?
   A) kisses them
   B) autographs their sleeve
   C) punches them
   D) shoots them

159) Why does Vesper Lynd (played by Ursula Andress) hire Evelyn Tremble?

A) so he can dress up in a variety of costumes at her flat
B) so he can practice the method described in his book, "How To Win At Baccarat"
C) so he can drive fast cars in high-speed chases
D) so he can play the bagpipes and take bubble baths

160) In *CASINO ROYALE,* Miss Goodthighs
A) is played by Jackie Bisset, who seduces Peter Sellers.
B) is played by Joanna Pettet, who pretends to be the daughter of Mata Hari and James Bond.
C) is played by Daliah Lavi, who is strapped naked to a table by Woody Allen.
D) is the name of a potent cocktail given to David Niven by Ursula Andress.

161) Although in the movie Le Chiffre is a KGB paymaster and expert card player, what else does he do to raise additional cash?
A) performs magic tricks and prestidigitation
B) sells wine and does voice-overs
C) sells blackmail pornographic photos of world leaders
D) deals in white slavery throughout the Third World

162) During the "Highlanders" sequence, who plays Richard Burton?
A) Richard Burton
B) Leslie Nielsen
C) Peter O'Toole
D) Peter Ustinov

163) Why does Vesper Lynd wear her "Elephant Boy" outfit—shocking pink with pink-blue feathers—only inside her "spy code room"?
A) People outside might stare.
B) It might fall apart with the slightest breeze.
C) It doesn't fit properly.
D) She never thinks to wear it outside.

164) TRUE or FALSE. There were so many different writers working on the screenplay of *CASINO ROYALE* that no one was com-

pletely sure who wrote what. Woody Allen even asked the producer, Charles K. Feldman, for a signed statement confirming that he, Woody, did none of the writing.

165) The girl in the compromising picture (see next page) is Daliah Lavi, who plays one of Sir James's secret agents. She's gambling in the Casino when Doctor Noah (played by Woody Allen) abducts her and has her strapped naked to this table. When asked why he does this to women, he replies
   A) that he learned it in the Boy Scouts.
   B) that he wants to show her that he is superior to his uncle, Sir James Bond.
   C) that this is the only way he can get someone to listen to him play Debussy.
   D) that he is anxious to replicate her body with one of his thousand doubles, and that he and "the double" have already enjoyed some "profoundly moving religious experiences" together.

166) What "looks like an aspirin, tastes like an aspirin, but isn't an aspirin"?
   A) cyanide
   B) Doctor Noah's baccillus
   C) a capsule containing 400 tiny little time pills
   D) a capsule containing vaporized lysergic acid

167) In the novel, 007 is apprehended by Le Chiffre and taken away for torture. What is the method of that torture?
   A) Bond is sent through a tunnel that has spiders, rats and a huge octopus waiting for him at the end.
   B) Bond is strapped naked into a seatless chair and repeatedly smacked on his bottom with a carpet beater.
   C) Bond is hooked up to an electronic device that alters his brainwaves.
   D) Bond and Vesper are tied together and dragged through the harbor off Royale-les-Eaux behind Le Chiffre's "bathosub."

(CREDIT: COLUMBIA PICTURES)

WOODY ALLEN and DALIAH LAVI

168) The climactic fight scene in the casino took two months to shoot and cost nearly a million dollars. It is a scene of constant chaos featuring all sorts of guest stars as well as various big-name international celebrities in cameo appearances. During the sequence, who says, "I've been framed. This gun shoots backwards. I just killed myself"?

A) Jean-Paul Belmondo
B) William Holden
C) George Raft
D) Edward G. Robinson

169) In order to make the office at the casino go up and down like an elevator, what must one do?

A) Stick a finger into a stuffed tiger.
B) Click your heels together three times and say, "There's no place like home."
C) Close the two-way mirror and face the casino.
D) Press the elevator button.

170) In the book, where does Bond hide the check for 70 million francs after he wins it from Le Chiffre?

A) under the floorboards in the bedroom of his suite (Room 44) at the Splendide
B) with Felix Leiter for safekeeping
C) under the dashboard of his Bentley, right next to the Colt Police Positive with the sawed-off barrel
D) behind the plastic number plate outside his hotel room door

13 THOSE LIPS, THOSE EYES . . .

171) In all the stories written by Ian Fleming, world-famous lover
James Bond sleeps only with
A) Vesper, Solitaire, Gala, Tiffany, Tatiana, Honey, Jill,
Pussy, Domino, Vivienne, Tracy and Kissy.
B) Vesper, Solitaire, Tiffany, Tatiana, Jill, Pussy, Domino,
Vivienne, Tracy and Kissy.
C) Vesper, Tiffany, Tatiana, Honey, Jill, Pussy, Domino, Vi-
vienne, Tracy, Mariko and Kissy.
D) all the women he encountered.

172) In the Bond films, 007 sleeps with ladies of all nationalities and
races. However, he only makes love to one virgin. In which film
does this landmark event occur?
A) *FROM RUSSIA WITH LOVE*
B) *YOU ONLY LIVE TWICE*
C) *LIVE AND LET DIE*
D) *FOR YOUR EYES ONLY*

173) Excluding *CASINO ROYALE* and *NEVER SAY NEVER
AGAIN,* how many women has 007 kissed in the movies?
A) 26
B) 37
C) 48
D) 86½

174) Which actress started her professional working career as a fare
collector on a bus line?
A) Shirley Eaton
B) Britt Ekland
C) Carole Bouquet
D) Mie Hama

175) Often those who spend a night with 007 don't live very long
afterwards. Some die in a horrible accident, others are killed by

the villain. In which films do women who've slept with Bond die for their troubles?

- A) *GOLDFINGER, THUNDERBALL, YOU ONLY LIVE TWICE, DIAMONDS ARE FOREVER, LIVE AND LET DIE, THE MAN WITH THE GOLDEN GUN,* and *MOONRAKER*
- B) *GOLDFINGER, YOU ONLY LIVE TWICE, LIVE AND LET DIE,* and *MOONRAKER*
- C) *GOLDFINGER, YOU ONLY LIVE TWICE, DIA-MONDS ARE FOREVER, LIVE AND LET DIE, THE MAN WITH THE GOLDEN GUN,* and *FOR YOUR EYES ONLY*
- D) *GOLDFINGER, THUNDERBALL, YOU ONLY LIVE TWICE, ON HER MAJESTY'S SECRET SERVICE, LIVE AND LET DIE, THE MAN WITH THE GOLDEN GUN, MOONRAKER,* and *FOR YOUR EYES ONLY*

176) Which female star did Cubby Broccoli once say "sounded like a Dutch comic" when she spoke?
- A) Ursula Andress
- B) Daniela Bianchi
- C) Claudine Auger
- D) Akiko Wakabayashi

177) In *THUNDERBALL,* at the Kiss Kiss nightclub, Bond dances with SPECTRE's beautiful chief of execution, Fiona Volpe. But during the dance, Fiona is shot in the back with a single bullet. To avoid a general panic, Bond
- A) carries her off with the flourish of a newly married man, excusing his "tired bride."
- B) sits her down and tells a nearby patron, "She's just dead."
- C) covers the wound with his finger and keeps dancing.
- D) hands her over to another SPECTRE operative, punches the guy in the stomach, and then races off through the crowd.

178) Where does Commander James Bond ask Countess Tracy di Vicenzo to marry him?
   A) in an abandoned farmhouse during a blizzard
   B) in a closed ski shop in the mountains
   C) in the car during the chase at a stock-car race
   D) during the lyrical love montage through Europe

179) James Bond and *Playboy* magazine have a long history of mutual relations. Six stories written by Ian Fleming appeared originally in the magazine, and three issues have featured major stories on the James Bond motion pictures. Of the following, which list contains the names of those ladies who did *not* display more than a smile in *Playboy?*
   A) Ursula Andress, Barbara Bach, Maud Adams
   B) Barbara Carrera, Kim Basinger, Lana Wood
   C) Mie Hama, Margaret Nolan, Martine Beswick
   D) Lois Chiles, Britt Ekland, Honor Blackman

180) The ladies who've fallen for Agent 007 in each of the movies come from a variety of professional backgrounds. Two of the women were stars in the English television series "The Avengers" prior to their Bond debuts. They were
   A) Claudine Auger
   B) Diana Rigg
   C) Karen Dor
   D) Honor Blackman

14 YOU ONLY LIVE TWICE

181) In what city is Bond "killed" in the pre-title sequence?
    A) Hong Kong
    B) Jakarta
    C) Macao
    D) Tokyo

182) Before 007 leaves for Japan, Miss Moneypenny gives him a book entitled *Instant Japanese*. Bond says he doesn't need it, reminding her that he "took a first" in Oriental languages at Cambridge. Why is this statement incorrect?
    A) He "took a second" in Oriental languages.
    B) He never studied Japanese.
    C) He never went to Cambridge.
    D) He never actually said this in the movie.

183) What is the name of the unfortunate American astronaut who gets cut loose during the space walk?
    A) Chris
    B) Dave
    C) Bob
    D) Mark

184) TRUE or FALSE. According to what we see on the screen, Siberia is a land of sunshine and palm trees.

185) The name of the actor pictured with Sean Connery in the photograph on the next page is Charles Gray. Although his part is cut short in *YOU ONLY LIVE TWICE* (apparently his appointment with destiny is on time), he does reappear in
    A) *DIAMONDS ARE FOREVER.*
    B) *LIVE AND LET DIE.*
    C) *THE MAN WITH THE GOLDEN GUN.*
    D) *NEVER SAY NEVER AGAIN.*

(CREDIT: WIDE WORLD PHOTOS)

SEAN CONNERY and CHARLES GRAY

186) Charles Gray's character, named Henderson, works for the British Secret Service until his death. Bond arrives at Gray's Oriental flat and, in order to make sure Henderson is who he claims to be,

    A) he asks Henderson to whistle a college fight song.

    B) he slams a wooden cane against Henderson's left leg.

    C) he slams a wooden cane against Henderson's right leg.

    D) he demands that Henderson recite the entire *Magna Carta* in reverse order.

187) TRUE or FALSE. Henderson offers Bond a drink, and prepares 007 his favorite vodka martini "stirred, not shaken."

188) In the novel, Bond travels to Japan to arrange an exchange of information with Tiger Tanaka of the Japanese Secret Service. _____ is the name of Tanaka's cover organization.

    A) The Koan-Chosa-Kyoku

    B) The Bureau of All-Asian Folkways

    C) The C.I.D.

    D) The Trembling-Leaf Parlor

AKIKO WAKABAYASHI

(CREDIT: DUFFY/ESQUIRE ASSOCIATES © 1967)

189) What is a "nightingale floor"?
- A) a material similar to tatami, used as the floor surface in sushi restaurants in Japan
- B) a special area in an Oriental house of prostitution, where 007 and Mariko Ichiban explore a very special Japanese art form
- C) a specially constructed floor guaranteed to make noise when you walk on it
- D) a surprise floor that disappears beneath James Bond, sending him tumbling through an underground steel shaft

190) When Bond first meets Aki (played by Akiko Wakabayashi and pictured above) in the wrestling auditorium, what words must they exchange with one another?
- A) "Do you have a light?"
- B) "I love you."
- C) "The Tiger knows all."
- D) "Hail, Tiger."

191) Where does Aki die?
- A) in bed with James Bond
- B) in the crossfire at the volcano

C) at the Ninja Training School

D) she doesn't die

192) In the novel, Dr. Guntram Shatterhand and his wife, Frau Emmy, both hold valid Swiss passports and live in a semi-ruined castle in Kyushu. Extremely wealthy horticulturists,

A) they live quietly unto themselves, and have only recently been accused of stealing bodies from a nearby graveyard.

B) they hire a staff of former "Black Dragons" to field a "Ninja Fighting Team" in the upcoming Olympics.

C) they develop a radar tracking system that enables them to intercept satellites passing over Japan, concealing the pirated satellites deep within their garden.

D) they create a garden known as the "Disneyland of Death."

193) Helga Brandt is going to torture Bond with _____ if he doesn't tell her who he is.

A) kindness

B) a dermitone

C) nitrous oxide

D) a synthetic turpentine solution

194) In the book, Blofeld captures Bond and puts him into one of Ian Fleming's favorite devices: a torture chair. What is the method used in this chair?

A) Electrodes are attached to his genitals.

B) A mask with a mouse inside is placed over his face.

C) Hot mud at 1,000° centigrade shoots up through a hole in the earth.

D) It holds Bond still while he is beaten senseless with a carpet beater, à la Le Chiffre.

195) Because he's James Bond, he manages to break free of the torture chair, of course, and pursues Blofeld through the castle. When he finally catches the old villain, how does Bond avenge the death of his wife, Tracy? (Remember, this is the novel. If you're paying attention, you know 007 hasn't even met Tracy in the movies yet.)

74

A) He drowns Blofeld in a vat of scalding peanut oil.

B) He throws Blofeld into a fumarole, where he's finished off by piranhas.

C) He chokes Blofeld to death with his bare hands.

D) He shoots Blofeld at point-blank range with his Walther.

196) The American spaceship _____ is about to go into its fourth orbit around the earth when SPECTRE's Intruder rocket swallows it up in outer space.

A) Jupiter 2

B) Jupiter 16

C) Gemini 8

D) Mercury 16

197) Pictured on the next page is the delightful Kissy Suzuki, played by Mie Hama. As part of the cover created for 007 by Tanaka, Bond "marries" Kissy in a full-fledged Oriental wedding. But why are they not officially married to one another?

A) They don't consummate their marriage.

B) Bond gives the priest a fake name.

C) Bond doesn't "marry" Kissy, he "marries" Aki.

D) The priest is an agent working for Tanaka, so the ceremony isn't officially sanctioned.

198) In the book, Kissy Suzuki is known as "the Japanese Garbo," a nickname given her after her only trip to Hollywood to appear in a motion picture. But what other character did Fleming once liken to Garbo?

A) Honeychile Rider

B) Tatiana Romanova

C) Jill Masterton

D) Tracy di Vicenzo

199) Who saves James Bond from almost certain death deep within the exploding volcano when Blofeld is about to shoot him?

A) Aki, who appears in her white Mustang, ready to drive 007 to safety

B) Kissy, who arrives with 100 Ninja Warriors

MIE HAMA

(CREDIT: DUFFY/ESQUIRE ASSOCIATES © 1967)

C) Tiger, who throws a "Ninja disc" into Blofeld's wrist
D) Kissy, who shoots Blofeld with a blowdart

200) Who has the last word in *YOU ONLY LIVE TWICE*?
A) James Bond
B) Miss Moneypenny
C) Kissy Suzuki
D) Tiger Tanaka

15 IT WAS SO BIG THAT . . .

201) Which was the largest set built for a James Bond film?
   A) the Taj Mahal used in *CASINO ROYALE*
   B) the volcano interior used in *YOU ONLY LIVE TWICE*
   C) the oil-tanker interior used in THE *SPY WHO LOVED ME*
   D) the space-station interior used in *MOONRAKER*

202) Who has designed the greatest number of James Bond films?
   A) Ken Adam
   B) Syd Cain
   C) Peter Lamont
   D) Peter Murton

203) TRUE or FALSE. The exterior of the real Fort Knox was used for location shooting in *GOLDFINGER*.

204) Blofeld's Institute of Physiological Research appears in
   A) *YOU ONLY LIVE TWICE.*
   B) *ON HER MAJESTY'S SECRET SERVICE.*
   C) *DIAMONDS ARE FOREVER.*
   D) *NEVER SAY NEVER AGAIN.*

205) TRUE or FALSE. Located atop Schilthorn Peak in Switzerland, the revolving restaurant pictured on the next page was named *Piz Gloria* and provided Ian Fleming with the inspiration for a new setting.

206) In which film are the walls of a main character's apartment composed of the Parthenon's original west wall as well as Bosch's "Garden of Delight"?
   A) *DOCTOR NO*
   B) *CASINO ROYALE*
   C) *ON HER MAJESTY'S SECRET SERVICE*
   D) *MOONRAKER*

Piz Gloria atop snow-covered mountain

(CREDIT: SWISS NAT'L TOURIST OFFICE)

207) During location shooting, the cast and crew of _____ traveled more than 100,000 miles, used more than 80 transport vehicles, consumed approximately 100,000 gallons of fuel, ate 10,800 pounds of meat and 26,000 rashers of bacon, and polished off 50,250 bottles of beer, wine and assorted soft drinks.
   A) *CASINO ROYALE*
   B) *THE SPY WHO LOVED ME*
   C) *MOONRAKER*
   D) *OCTOPUSSY*

208) In which production did a lack of snowfall require seven large trucks to make 45 trips to nearby peaks to bring in enough snow that shooting could continue?
   A) *ON HER MAJESTY'S SECRET SERVICE*
   B) *THE SPY WHO LOVED ME*
   C) *FOR YOUR EYES ONLY*
   D) None: these are fictional statistics.

209) In which film did the large, rusting hulk of the ocean liner *Queen Elizabeth* appear?
   A) *DOCTOR NO*
   B) *THUNDERBALL*
   C) *YOU ONLY LIVE TWICE*
   D) *THE MAN WITH THE GOLDEN GUN*

210) TRUE or FALSE. The ceremonial barge that carries Octopussy across the lake in India was actually loaned to the production team by the Maharajah of Udaipur, who also granted the Bond team permission to film all over "the City of Sunrise."

211) What is our first glimpse of George Lazenby as James Bond?
   A) He's lighting a cigarette.
   B) He's standing on the beach and says, "My name is Bond, James Bond."
   C) He's at a card table in Portugal.
   D) He's in bed with Tracy.

212) What car does 007 drive in *ON HER MAJESTY'S SECRET SERVICE?*
   A) an Aston Martin DB II
   B) an Aston Martin DB III
   C) an Aston Martin DB V
   D) an Aston Martin DB VI

213) TRUE or FALSE. George Lazenby was a model with no acting experience when he was cast in *ON HER MAJESTY'S SECRET SERVICE.* He got in to see producer Harry Saltzman without reading a line of dialogue and was cast in the part after bloodying the nose of a stuntman.

GEORGE LAZENBY

(COURTESY OF ARTIST)

214) TRUE or FALSE. While portraying the character of Sir Hilary Bray, the Australian Lazenby based his perfectly "English" gentleman's accent upon that of television personality David Frost.

215) During the opening credits, an attempt is made to remind audiences that even though there's a new man playing 007, it still is a real James Bond picture. A series of cinematic images from past films creep through the Maurice Binder credits, and we see a whole bunch of familiar faces. Whom don't we see?
   A) Ursula Andress
   B) Joseph Wiseman
   C) Gert Frobe
   D) Harold Sakata

216) How much sex does Tracy feel she owes Bond for bailing her out at the casino?
   A) 3,000 francs worth
   B) 5,000 francs worth
   C) 10,000 francs worth
   D) She doesn't feel she owes him anything.

217) Draco's men finally abduct 007. As Bond is being led into Marc-Ange Draco's office, what does he hear?
   A) a midget whistling "Goldfinger"
   B) a gunshot going off
   C) squeals of delight through the door
   D) a radio playing "Fly Me To The Moon"

218) *Herkos Odonton* is the classical Greek equivalant of
   A) "on your honor"
   B) "I do for you, you do for me"
   C) "the hedge of the teeth"
   D) "for your eyes only"

219) In the film, why does 007 try to resign from the Secret Service?
   A) He's "had it" with Moneypenny's flirtatious ways.
   B) He's been taken off Operation Bedlam and still hasn't found Blofeld.

C) He's been forced to confine all his duties to Operation Bedlam, in what he believes to be a futile search for Blofeld.

D) He's been turned down for a two-week leave of absence, and has just "had it" with "M."

220) According to Sable Basilisk, what would be the one distinguishing physical characteristic of the *real* "Count de Bleuchamp"?
A) no earlobes
B) a hairlip
C) a bump on the bridge of his nose
D) no hair on his head or eyebrows

221) When Bond visits "M" at home, we learn that the old admiral
A) collects butterflies.
B) is a numismatist.
C) is a philatelist.
D) is a teetotaler.

222) Where does Bond want to take Blofeld in order to verify certain family records regarding Blofeld's claim to the title "Count de Bleuchamp"?
A) Augsburg
B) Galicia
C) Krakow
D) Vienna

223) Who tells Tracy that James Bond might only be interested in her because Draco is willing to pay him one million pounds for that interest?
A) Nancy
B) Ruby
C) Olympe
D) Zara

224) In the novel *ON HER MAJESTY'S SECRET SERVICE,* we learn for the first time quite a bit about the mysterious past of James Bond. We learn that his family motto is "The World Is Not Enough," and that

A) he was tossed out of Eton for various difficulties with the headmaster and his wife.

B) he lived with his aunt, Charmain, in Pett Bottom.

C) his father was Scottish and his mother was Swiss.

D) his first love was a woman named Marthe de Brandt.

225) What does Ruby do to 007 under the table?
A) She dresses up like a French poodle and teaches Bond tricks.
B) She impresses him with her sexual skills.
C) She writes on his flesh with lipstick.
D) She intertwines her leg with his, nudging his "wedding tackle."

226) Bond tells one of the girls at dinner, "It has four balls, if you'd care to see it." What is he talking about?
A) a game
B) a herald
C) a circus performer
D) a photograph

227) What is the name of the game played by Bond and the girls on the roof of Blofeld's headquarters?
A) curling
B) icing
C) skitting
D) sloshing

228) When and where are James Bond and Tracy di Vicenzo (played by Diana Rigg) married?
A) Christmas Eve, Geneva, Switzerland
B) Christmas Day, Bonn, West Germany
C) New Year's Eve, Estoril, Portugal
D) New Year's Day, Munich, West Germany

229) What does 007 do when Marc-Ange Draco gives him a check for marrying Draco's daughter?

A) He gives it back to him.

B) He takes it and tears it up when Draco isn't looking.

C) He tells Draco the name of his bank, but tells Tracy that he'll transfer it to a charity as soon as possible.

D) He tells Draco to keep his money, that he'll let his new father-in-law help out with their children's education.

230) The last shot in *ON HER MAJESTY'S SECRET SERVICE* is

A) of a close-up of James Bond weeping.

B) of a bullet hole in the windshield.

C) of Bond holding a dead Tracy in his arms.

D) of the Aston Martin on the side of the road, still decorated from the wedding.

DIANA RIGG and GEORGE LAZENBY cut their wedding cake   (CREDIT: GLOBE PHOTOS)

17 ANOTHER OPENING, ANOTHER SHOW

231) The premiere of _____ caused riots in the streets of Boston.
   A) *DOCTOR NO*
   B) *CASINO ROYALE*
   C) *DIAMONDS ARE FOREVER*
   D) *NEVER SAY NEVER AGAIN*

232) Two hundred sleepy patrons were treated to breakfast by the management of an Asbury Park movie house when they arrived at 4 A.M. to view _____ during a 24-hour run of the film. Tickets sold for $1.49 at each performance.
   A) *GOLDFINGER*
   B) *THUNDERBALL*
   C) *YOU ONLY LIVE TWICE*
   D) *DIAMONDS ARE FOREVER*

233) Which film was banned in Israel after running for six weeks?
   A) *FROM RUSSIA WITH LOVE*
   B) *GOLDFINGER*
   C) *CASINO ROYALE*
   D) *FOR YOUR EYES ONLY*

234) TRUE or FALSE. The only James Bond film ever shown in the Soviet Union was *FROM RUSSIA WITH LOVE.*

235) Soon after *GOLDFINGER* opened, boutiques and clothing stores began stocking all sorts of "James Bond" items. Gold-bordered handkerchiefs, 007 cuff links and special rain coats and pajamas all contributed to the fashion craze of the mid-1960s. In fact, all this attention led the leading fashion magazines of _____ to label Bond "the Don Juan of 1965."
   A) Brazil
   B) France
   C) Italy
   D) Spain

236) The newspapers of what country nicknamed James Bond "Mr. Bang Bang Kiss Kiss"?
    A) France
    B) Italy
    C) Japan
    D) United States

237) *MOONRAKER,* the most expensive James Bond film ever made, cost _____ more than *DOCTOR NO,* the least expensive film.
    A) 5 times
    B) 10 times
    C) 30 times
    D) 40 times

238) Which Bond movie has been seen by the most people around the world?
    A) *GOLDFINGER*
    B) *THUNDERBALL*
    C) *THE SPY WHO LOVED ME*
    D) *MOONRAKER*

239) The poster artwork advertising *FOR YOUR EYES ONLY* features Roger Moore aiming his gun between the sexy legs of a lady holding a crossbow. Despite the furor over whose legs were actually featured in the ads, two major city newspapers cropped the eye-popping design from the knees up. Which two papers performed this surgery?
    A) the Boston *Globe*
    B) the Los Angeles *Times*
    C) the New York *Times*
    D) the San Francisco *Chronicle*

240) Each James Bond movie opens the same way: the screen is dark, we hear the pulsating music of the "James Bond Theme," 007 appears walking across the screen in the sights of a gun barrel, he turns and fires at the camera, and red blood drips down the

screen until the white dot of the gunsight vanishes. Who came up with this cinematic tradition?

A) Maurice Binder
B) Albert R. Broccoli
C) Robert Brownjohn
D) Harry Saltzman

18 DIAMONDS ARE FOREVER

241) In the novel, the Spangled Mob runs a diamond-smuggling operation all over the world. Operating racetracks in Saratoga and gambling joints in Las Vegas, they stretch their interests far and wide. But how do they smuggle the diamonds out of the South African mines?

A) A dentist, who is on the payroll, extracts diamonds from the wide-open mouths of the miners, pays the miners and passes the diamonds along.

B) The miners swallow the diamonds and, each evening, must travel a great distance to a special doctor who pumps their stomachs.

C) One of DeBeer's foremen is a lieutenant in Serrafimo Spang's gang.

D) The miners carefully place one or two stones within the carcass of a giant scorpion, and sell the furry pelts at auction to a special wholesaler who takes them to London.

242) While the film's pre-title sequence features a deadly mud bath for Ernst Stavro Blofeld, mud is used differently in the novel. How is it used?

A) Tiffany and Bond roll around in the mud outside Spang's ghost town, as 007 tries to get her defenses down.

B) Bond is once again strapped into a seatless chair that is positioned over a mud geyser that's about to explode.

C) 007 takes a restorative mud bath at the racetrack, and is buried under too much mud to be able to prevent a murder from taking place in the baths.

D) Bond and Felix Leiter travel to a "mud factory," which is nothing more than a front for a diamond-processing plant.

243) After the opening credits, we see Bond and "M" learning all about diamonds at the home of Sir Donald Munger, noted diamond expert. During the lecture, Bond shows off his knowledge by

A) explaining the smuggling system even before Sir Donald has a chance to speak, throwing "M" into a tizzy.

B) identifying the size and cut of each diamond in Munger's private collection.

C) sniffing a glass of sherry and identifying both its name and its vintage.

D) sniffing a glass of Mouton Cadet and identifying both its vintage and the winemaster who tended the casks in France where it was made.

244) Pictured on the next page with James Bond is Jill St. John, who plays Tiffany Case in *DIAMONDS ARE FOREVER*. When Bond arrives at her Amsterdam flat and identifies himself as Peter Franks, what does she do?
   A) gives him a medal
   B) checks his glass for fingerprints
   C) checks his cigarette case for fingerprints
   D) telephones someone and cancels a date

245) In the novel, why is Tiffany reluctant to sleep with Bond?
   A) She wants to stay a virgin.
   B) She doesn't find 007 sexually appealing.
   C) She was gang-raped when she was 16 years old.
   D) She is still too much of a drunkard, and even has the nickname "the Pickled Relish."

246) At Circus, Circus in Las Vegas, what does Tiffany do to get the diamonds?
   A) offers herself as a prize
   B) plays an unenthusiastic game of water balloon
   C) dresses up like a monkey and scares little children
   D) wins three hands at poker

247) At yet another casino, Tiffany finds Desmond Llewellyn and shouts, "Hiya, Mister Q" when the armorer is playing the slots. She asks how he keeps winning, and he says he
   A) is not winning.
   B) would rather be in London.

SEAN CONNERY with JILL ST. JOHN (CREDIT: GLOBE PHOTOS)

    C)   is using the powers taught him by Uri Geller.
    D)   is testing out a new r.p.m. controller.

248)   Although Bond is in the United States throughout most of *DIA-MONDS ARE FOREVER* and is forced to use Tiffany's tiny Mustang convertible, when or where do we see his famous Aston Martin?
    A)   in the opening pre-credits sequence
    B)   as he crosses the customs border for the hydrofoil
    C)   at "Q" branch, as his car is being fitted with enormous rockets
    D)   outside Tiffany's Amsterdam flat

249)   In the novel, what does Bond use to smuggle the diamonds into the United States?
    A)   a corpse
    B)   golf balls

C) a bible with a cut-out center

D) the British diplomatic pouch

250) What is a "Brooklyn Stomping"?
A) something unpleasant involving football cleats and a human body
B) tailgate parties for horse-racing fans
C) a dance that Tiffany teaches to Bond before they make love
D) what 007 gives to Mr. Wint and Mr. Kidd aboard the *Queen Elizabeth*

251) Where *doesn't* the novel *DIAMONDS ARE FOREVER* take place?
A) Saratoga Racetrack
B) the Tiara Casino
C) the Acme Mud and Sulpher Baths
D) the Slumber Funeral Home

252) When Bond receives an urn containing diamonds, he's at the Slumber Funeral Home. What is the name of the man who runs the place?
A) Melvin Slumber
B) Morton Slumber
C) Martin Slumber
D) Myron Slumber

253) Dean Martin's uncle, stand-up comic Leonard Barr, plays
A) Mr. Wint.
B) Mr. Kidd.
C) Shady Tree.
D) Burt Saxby.

254) Of the following performers, who was signed to appear in the movie but was cut out at the last minute?
A) Joey Bishop
B) Sammy Davis, Jr.

C) Jerry Lewis
D) Don Rickles

255) The word "Spectreville" appears in the book. What does it mean?
   A) It's the name given to the first training facility used by Ernst Stavro Blofeld.
   B) It's a mountaintop resort near Lake Tahoe.
   C) It's an abandoned community in the Spectre Mountain Range.
   D) It's 1950s lingo for a place that has the "evil eye" looking down upon it.

256) While gambling at the crap table inside "the Whyte House," a girl comes up to 007 and says, "Hi, I'm Plenty." What happens to her?
   A) She gets beaten and raped.
   B) She gets tossed ten stories to her death wearing only her panties.
   C) She gets tossed into a pool from Bond's window, wearing only panties and shoes.
   D) She disappears from the story, eventually surfacing as a star on an American daytime soap opera.

257) Bond arrives at the summer home of Willard Whyte, only to be met by these two hot-tempered vixens (see next page). What are their names and who plays them?
   A) Bambi is played by Trina Parks; Thumper is played by Donna Garratt.
   B) Pyramus is played by Margaret Lacey; Thisby is played by Lana Wood.
   C) Heckle is played by Donna Garratt; Jeckle is played by Trina Parks.
   D) Thumper is played by Trina Parks; Bambi is played by Donna Garratt.

258) TRUE or FALSE. The girls almost succeed in drowning James Bond in Whyte's pool, until Felix arrives in the nick of time with the FBI.

Bond battles two hot-tempered vixens

(CREDIT: UPI)

259) A cassette containing the correct coding information programs the space laser. Blofeld keeps the cassette in an unassuming case with the name _____ printed on it.
   A) "World's Greatest Marches"
   B) "World's Greatest Themes"
   C) "World's Greatest Military Marches"
   D) "World's Greatest Sambas"

260) Although Blofeld is smashed about in his "bathosub" at the climax of the film, screenwriter Richard Maibaum had written a different ending in which the villain's fate would be sealed. It was supposed to be
   A) a death-defying race across Mount Rushmore.
   B) a boat race across Lake Mead to Hoover Dam.
   C) a fistfight at the La Brea Tar Pits, where the villain would sink beneath the ooze.
   D) a hair-raising chase across the rim of the Grand Canyon.

19 THERE'S A PLACE FOR US, SOMEWHERE

261) In *FROM RUSSIA WITH LOVE,* Bond and Tatiana board the Orient Express for points north. At what station along the route does Red Grant board the train, introducing himself to 007 as a member of the British Secret Service?
   A) Belgrade
   B) Sarajevo
   C) Trieste
   D) Zagreb

262) Supposedly located near the coast of mainland China, Scaramanga's hideout in *THE MAN WITH THE GOLDEN GUN* is actually a location off the coast of Thailand (see the next page). What is its real name?
   A) Aah Sohl
   B) Buriram
   C) Sakon
   D) Phuket

263) TRUE or FALSE. The climactic circus sequence in *OCTOPUSSY,* wherein 007 saves Europe from a nuclear explosion, was filmed at an actual U.S. Air Force base in West Germany.

264) "Laughing Water"
   A) is the name of the estate used in the shooting of *DOCTOR NO.*
   B) is the nickname given the shark set used in *THUNDERBALL.*
   C) is the name of the Injun Chief bomber used in *CASINO ROYALE.*
   D) is the original name of the ship used as the model for the "Flying Saucer" in *NEVER SAY NEVER AGAIN.*

265) Which film opens with a murder inside the United Nations (see page 98), and what is the method of that murder?

96

(CREDIT: TOURISM AUTHORITY OF THAILAND)

United Nations from the east

(CREDIT: UN PHOTO BY MILTON GRANT)

A) *YOU ONLY LIVE TWICE:* The ambassador is poisoned.

B) *ON HER MAJESTY'S SECRET SERVICE:* A secretary is stabbed.

C) *LIVE AND LET DIE:* An ambassador is killed with high-frequency sound waves.

D) *THE MAN WITH THE GOLDEN GUN:* A scientist is shot on the floor of the General Assembly.

266) After suffering the stares of over a thousand curious onlookers, the director of one Bond picture realized that he would get the location shot he needed only if he provided a suitable distraction for the star-struck populace. So after lunch he sent one of the company stuntmen across the street to hang from a third-floor balcony, screaming and waving for help. It worked. For which film was this ploy used?

A) *FROM RUSSIA WITH LOVE*

B) *ON HER MAJESTY'S SECRET SERVICE*

C) *LIVE AND LET DIE*

D) *FOR YOUR EYES ONLY*

267) During the shooting of *FOR YOUR EYES ONLY,* what happened at the monastery known as Meteora (pictured on the next page) that almost halted production?

A) The monks set fire to themselves during the shooting of the film.

B) The monks began selling souveniers to to the crew, regaling them with off-color stories.

C) The monks put up toilet paper and sheets around the place to prevent filming.

D) The single rope-operated elevator kept breaking down.

268) When we first see the headquarters of the British Secret Service in *DOCTOR NO,* it's located at Regent's Park—where Ian Fleming originally put it. By the time of *OCTOPUSSY,* however, the Service's main office

A) is still located in the same drab building.

B) has moved to Cambridge Circus.

Meteora, Thessaly, Greece

(CREDIT: GREEK NAT'L TOURIST OFFICE)

C) has moved to Oxford Street.
D) has moved to Whitehall.

269) In which film did the producers pay the local population over $100,000 to appear as extras during location shooting?
A) *CASINO ROYALE*
B) *YOU ONLY LIVE TWICE*
C) *THE MAN WITH THE GOLDEN GUN*
D) *OCTOPUSSY*

270) In which film does James Bond cross through "Checkpoint Charlie" on his way to the East?
A) *FROM RUSSIA WITH LOVE*
B) *CASINO ROYALE*
C) *FOR YOUR EYES ONLY*
D) *OCTOPUSSY*

"Checkpoint Charlie," West Berlin, Germany

(CREDIT: GERMAN INFORMATION CENTER)

20 *LIVE AND LET DIE*

271) The first time we see Roger Moore in *LIVE AND LET DIE*
   A) he's in bed in the arms of a girl.
   B) he's running down the street in hot pursuit of one of Mr. Big's hit men, whom he's just seen stabbing a CIA agent.
   C) he's playing *chemin de fer* at a London casino.
   D) he's making coffee for "M" with his home-brewing system.

272) *LIVE AND LET DIE* is the second Bond novel written by Ian Fleming. In it, 007 undergoes a skin graft before setting out for Jamaica. Why does "Q" branch put him through this?
   A) He has burned himself on the testing range while firing an experimental flamethrower.
   B) He has recently received an exploding package in his hotel room that badly injured his shoulder.
   C) A spy cannot walk around with any distinguishing features, and 007 now has a *second* scar.
   D) The Secret Service is experimenting with plastic surgery and thinks it time Bond looked like someone other than Hoagy Carmichael.

273) Mr. Big smuggles heroin in the movie, but he smuggles _____ in the book.
   A) heroin
   B) cigarettes and rum
   C) Bloody Morgan's buried treasure
   D) poisonous scorpions, octopi and opium

274) A character not appearing in the novel but used in the film is named after one of the technical advisors to the movie. Which one?
   A) the boat operator.
   B) the crocodile trainer.
   C) the driver of the double-decker bus.
   D) the kite-flying expert.

DAVID HEDISON as Felix Leiter

(COURTESY OF ARTIST)

275) When Felix Leiter (played by David Hedison) appears on the screen, he bears no resemblance to the man described in the book. And by the end of the novel, Felix's outward appearance has changed dramatically. What happens to Felix in the book?
   A) He is chewed on by a shark.
   B) He loses an arm to the Robber during a fight with a chain saw.
   C) He is chewed on by a hungry alligator.
   D) He is caught underneath a speeding motorboat somewhere in the Florida Everglades.

276) "Trespassers Will Be Eaten" is the sign referring to
   A) the Ourobourous Worm and Bait Shippers factory.
   B) an alligator farm.
   C) a crocodile farm.
   D) the picnic grounds on the isle of San Monique.

277) What was the route number on the British Transport double-decker bus that served as the green "San Monique Transport" stolen by 007?
   A) No. 1
   B) No. 3

C) No. 19

D) No. 24

278) In the advertising artwork for *LIVE AND LET DIE*, the new 007 was surrounded by four Tarot cards. What were they?
   A) The Fool, The Priestess, The Lovers, Death
   B) The Devil, Death, The Lovers, The Wheel of Fortune
   C) The Fool, Death, The Devil, The Queen of Cups
   D) The Wheel of Fortune, The Lovers, Death, The High Priestess

279) Who played Mr. Big?
   A) Earl Johnny Brown
   B) Julius W. Harris
   C) Yaphet Kotto
   D) Roy Stewart

280) In the book, when Bond and Leiter arrive at "the Boneyard" in Harlem,
   A) nightclub stripper G-G Sumatra does her exotic show as 007 and Felix disappear, along with their table, through the floor.
   B) the cab driver who drove them there telephones Mr. Big and lets him know that they've arrived.
   C) they begin asking questions regarding the whereabouts of Mr. Big, but no one in the Harlem club has anything to say to the two white men.
   D) nothing happens, so they make their way to "the Filet Of Soul."

281) How does James Bond escape from a tiny island that is surrounded by "potential overnight bags"?
   A) He "attracts" a nearby rowboat to the island, with the aid of his magnetic wristwatch.
   B) He knifes one animal through the gut, making it an attractive meal (and diversion) for the others, and he swims ashore.
   C) He sets fire to the island, scaring away the animals, thus

James Bond and Solitaire

(CREDIT: UPI)

permitting him the freedom to reach the rowboat and get ashore.

D) He races across the backs of the reptiles when they conveniently line up next to one another and allow him to reach the shoreline.

282) On page 105, James Bond is protecting Solitaire from the worshippers of Baron Samedi. Solitaire, played by Jane Seymour, is a girl who can tell the future by reading Tarot cards, so even before she meets 007, she knows about him. As he prepares to leave London for New York City, she reads her cards and predicts certain things about Bond's trip. Of the following, what *doesn't* she predict?
A) ". . . a man comes . . ."
B) ". . . he travels quickly . . ."
C) ". . . he will oppose . . ."
D) ". . . he brings danger . . ."

283) TRUE or FALSE. After Bond spends the night in her bed, Solitaire tells him, "Physical violation cannot be undone," and proceeds to weep.

284) How does Bond convince Solitaire that they are destined to become lovers?
A) He buys a rigged deck of Tarot cards.
B) He tells her the truth, and she can "sense it."
C) He's nice to her after Kananga beats her, and she says she's always depended on the kindness of strangers. . . .
D) He reads the tarot cards while sitting in her special chair, and she believes he has the power, "just like I do."

285) Who is Quarrel, Jr.?
A) the Cayman Islander who is assigned to train Bond underwater in the novel
B) the soft-spoken henchman of Mr. Big who's from the "Lung Block" in New York City, where, because of all

the noise and smoke from surrounding factories, he had to shout all the time

C) the character in the movie *LIVE AND LET DIE,* so named because the original Quarrel (who appears in the book) already died in the movie *DOCTOR NO*

D) the man with the steel claw who almost breaks 007's finger and fights with him aboard the train ride to New York

286) He is the black FBI agent who saved Bond's neck up in Harlem. He is played by Lon Satton. His name is
A) Dambala.
B) Hendry.
C) Strutter.
D) Walker.

287) Who asks Bond if she can interest him in "something in heads"?
A) Miss Caruso
B) Rosie Carver
C) the salesgirl
D) the hotel desk clerk

288) The character of Sheriff J.W. Pepper (see the next page) appears in two films, *LIVE AND LET DIE* and *THE MAN WITH THE GOLDEN GUN.* This professional law enforcement agent from the Louisiana State Police Department is played by
A) James Cossins.
B) Clifton James.
C) Jerry Comeaux.
D) Gerald James.

289) What is the name of the band that plays during the funeral procession off Docker Street in New Orleans?
A) The Brother Love Band
B) The Olympia Brass Band
C) The Orleans Brass Band
D) The New Line Brass Band

Sheriff J.W. Pepper

(COURTESY OF ARTIST)

290) Who is Mr. Big/Dr. Kananga working for?
   A) Haile Selassie's government
   B) the Russians
   C) SPECTRE
   D) himself

21 I'VE GROWN ACCUSTOMED TO THAT FACE

291) Although we've come to know him more recently as General Gogol, Walter Gotell appeared in an earlier Bond film. What is the film and whom does he play?
   A) Playdell-Smith in *DOCTOR NO*
   B) Morzeny in *FROM RUSSIA WITH LOVE*
   C) Tousaint in *ON HER MAJESTY'S SECRET SERVICE*
   D) General Boris in *YOU ONLY LIVE TWICE*

292) TRUE or FALSE. The Armorer "Q," played by Desmond Llewelyn, appears with a car, gadget or weapon in every one of the James Bond films produced by Eon Productions.

293) Actor Shane Rimmer plays the part of Captain Carter in *THE SPY WHO LOVED ME*. He also appears in
   A) *YOU ONLY LIVE TWICE* and *DIAMONDS ARE FOREVER.*
   B) *YOU ONLY LIVE TWICE* and *LIVE AND LET DIE.*
   C) *GOLDFINGER, YOU ONLY LIVE TWICE* and *LIVE AND LET DIE.*
   D) *YOU ONLY LIVE TWICE, DIAMONDS ARE FOREVER* and *MOONRAKER.*

294) Geoffrey Keen appears in *THE SPY WHO LOVED ME, MOON-RAKER, FOR YOUR EYES ONLY* and *OCTOPUSSY* as
   A) the chief of staff.
   B) the minister of defense.
   C) an assistant in "Q" branch.
   D) the man who gives Bond his cars.

295) She plays Miss Moneypenny in 13 James Bond films, and currently writes a column called "Moneypenny" three times a week for a Canadian newspaper. Her name is
   A) Vivian Blaine.
   B) Lois Maxwell.

C) Lori Maxwell.

D) Lois Maxim.

296) In *FROM RUSSIA WITH LOVE,* two girls fight tooth and nail at the gypsy camp. Aliza Gur plays one of the wrestlers, and she has yet to reappear in a Bond film. But the other girl reappears in a later Bond movie in an altogether different type of role. Name the actress and her other Bond picture.

A) Nadja Regin, in *THUNDERBALL*

B) Martine Beswick, in *THUNDERBALL*

C) Margaret Nolan, in *YOU ONLY LIVE TWICE*

D) Zena Marshall, in *GOLDFINGER*

297) Felix Leiter is the CIA operative who is one of James Bond's oldest and closest friends. The character appears in six Bond films, but is never played by the same actor twice. Match the actor to the film.

A) Norman Burton

1) *DIAMONDS ARE FOREVER*

B) Bernie Casey

2) *DOCTOR NO*

C) David Hedison

3) *GOLDFINGER*

D) Cec Linder

4) *LIVE AND LET DIE*

E) Jack Lord

5) *NEVER SAY NEVER AGAIN*

F) Rik Van Nutter

6) *THUNDERBALL*

298) Which member of the James Bond cast appears in all of the following movies: *THE THIRD MAN, THE FALLEN IDOL, THE SPY WHO CAME IN FROM THE COLD* and *THE L-SHAPED ROOM?*

A) Desmond Llewelyn

B) Bernard Lee

C) Geoffrey Keen

D) Robert Brown

299) The following actors and actresses appear in more than one James Bond film, playing a different part in each movie. Match the performer's name with the titles of the Bond films they were in.

110

A)	George Baker	1)	*FROM RUSSIA WITH LOVE, GOLDFINGER*
B)	Robert Brown	2)	*CASINO ROYALE, ON HER MAJESTY'S SECRET SERVICE*
C)	Bert Kwok	3)	*THE SPY WHO LOVED ME, OCTOPUSSY*
D)	Marc Lawrence	4)	*MOONRAKER, FOR YOUR EYES ONLY*
E)	Nadja Regin	5)	*DIAMONDS ARE FOREVER, THE MAN WITH THE GOLDEN GUN*
F)	Angela Scoular	6)	*GOLDFINGER, YOU ONLY LIVE TWICE*
G)	Lizzie Warville	7)	*FOR YOUR EYES ONLY, OCTOPUSSY*
H)	Alison Worth	8)	*ON HER MAJESTY'S SECRET SERVICE, THE SPY WHO LOVED ME*

300) Charles Gray plays Blofeld in *DIAMONDS ARE FOREVER*. He also appears in another Bond film as
    A) a man who gets stabbed in the back.
    B) a man who warns of impending doom.
    C) a man who gets blown up inside a huge warehouse.
    D) a man who pretends to be working with the British.

301) *THE MAN WITH THE GOLDEN GUN* was the last full-length
novel written by Ian Fleming. It followed *YOU ONLY LIVE
TWICE* and was published after Fleming's death. In the opening
pages, James Bond, who has been missing for over a year, suddenly turns up in London. What happened to Bond during the
few months he spent under the care of "Colonel Boris" in Lenin-
grad?
   A)   He learned all the secrets about the KGB and was ready
        to tell London everything.
   B)   He was brainwashed and instructed to kill "M."
   C)   He was made to pay dearly for the deaths of Rosa Klebb
        and Red Grant.
   D)   Kissy Suzuki gave birth to 007's child, and the Russians
        brought the child to Bond in Leningrad.

302) In *THE MAN WITH THE GOLDEN GUN* we finally learn what
"M" 's real name is. He is officially known as
   A)   Admiral Sir Miles Mandish.
   B)   Admiral Sir Miles Messervy.
   C)   Admiral Sir Miles Molony.
   D)   Admiral Sir Mike Maloney.

303) Bond finally convinces the Secret Service that he may, in fact,
really be who he claims to be, so he is brought to "the soft room"
in Kensington Cloisters for interogation. Afterwards, he arrives
at the Secret Service Headquarters, where he's greeted by "M"
and Bill Tanner. What two actions of 007 alert the chief of staff
he's not the man he used to be?
   A)   He asks for a martini but requests gin instead of vodka,
        and he doesn't toss his hat onto the hat-hook in Money-
        penny's office.
   B)   He doesn't smoke his famous Morland specials, nor does
        he know who Maria Freudenstein is.
   C)   He doesn't have time to have lunch with Bill, nor does he
        smoke his famous cigarettes.

D)   He doesn't inquire about Mary Goodnight, nor does he remember the "Le Chiffre incident."

304)   In the movie, before sending Bond on his mission, "M" tells a somewhat inquisitive 007 that there are many people who might want the British spy dead. Aside from the Russians, who does "M" not mention?
A)   humiliated tailors
B)   outraged chefs
C)   jealous husbands
D)   frustrated bartenders

305)   TRUE or FALSE. When Bond pays a visit to the private estate of Hai Fat, he is greeted by a nude girl in a swimming pool, named "Chew Me."

306)   Where does Bond find the golden bullet used to kill Bill Fairbanks, Agent 002?
A)   in a girl's bellybutton
B)   in "Q" branch
C)   in the workshop of Lazar, the arms manufacturer
D)   he never finds it

307)   TRUE or FALSE. In the novel, Bond watches as the body of Mary Goodnight is run over by Scaramanga's private train.

308)   Who plays Mary Goodnight (pictured with Roger Moore on the next page)?
A)   Maud Adams
B)   Britt Ekland
C)   Jane Seymour
D)   Lana Wood

309)   Bond and Goodnight are finally about to spend the night together in 007's bed (after much coaxing and flirting by Mary). But when Andrea arrives unannounced, what happens?
A)   They enjoy a spontaneous threesome.
B)   Andrea apologizes for interrupting and leaves.

James Bond and Mary Goodnight

(CREDIT: UPI)

C) Goodnight hides in 007's closet for two hours.

D) Goodnight hides under the bed for three hours.

310) When is James Bond "arrested" under Section 403 by Lieutenant Hip, and brought out to visit "M" aboard a sunken ship?
A) never
B) after Gibson is murdered outside the "Bottoms Up" club
C) after Andrea is murdered inside the boxing arena
D) after Goodnight is trapped inside Scaramanga's trunk

311) TRUE or FALSE. In *THE MAN WITH THE GOLDEN GUN,* James Bond pushes a young Thai boy off a boat.

312) What is the solex agitator?
A) a new kind of washing machine
B) an Oriental improvement of the old brass knuckle, designed to cause severe internal bleeding
C) a vital piece of an energy conversion system
D) a laser-beam activated guidance system developed by Scaramanga

313) Who saves Bond from a mass of karate experts at the training school?
A) Lieutenant Hip's two young nieces
B) the Hong Kong Police and a red-neck sheriff
C) Nick Nack and the two Sumo wrestlers
D) He isn't saved. He's knocked unconscious and brought to Scaramanga's island.

314) Bond is challenged to a duel by Scaramanga (he really has no choice, because his plane has been destroyed), who will pit the golden gun of his own design against 007's Walther PPK. Scaramanga, who has an assortment of nicknames, wants to demonstrate who is the better shot. Of the following, which *isn't* a name he shoots by?
A) Francisco
B) Paco
C) Pistols
D) Bullets

<small>(CREDIT: WIDE WORLD PHOTOS)</small>

CHRISTOPHER LEE and ROGER MOORE prepare for duel

315) The climactic duel soon moves inside Scaramanga's "fun house."
Although Scaramanga has practiced inside the house many times,
007 (naturally) outwits him. What clue tells the audience that
Roger Moore is really standing where the dummy stood moments
before?
   A) We see Bond remove the dummy and stand in its place.
   B) We see Bond on Nick Nack's hidden television monitor,
       getting into place.
   C) Mary Goodnight tosses a fake gun to distract Scara-
       manga, allowing Bond to move into place.
   D) The previously blown-off fingers on the dummy are now
       replaced with real ones.

316) TRUE or FALSE. After disguising himself with a fake third
nipple, Bond arrives at Hai Fat's estate and convinces the old
industrialist that he, Bond, is the real "man with the golden gun."

317) Where does Bond stumble across J.W. Pepper?
   A) inside an American Motors dealership in Thailand
   B) inside a McDonald's in Macao

C) outside a porno shop in Hong Kong

D) riding a taxi through Bangkok

318) Why is Bond almost killed trying to retrieve the solex?

A) It doesn't belong to him and the owners are pretty pissed off.

B) Goodnight almost knocks him into the atomic cooling vats.

C) Nick Nack guides Bond back into the "fun house," where gangsters from the 1920s start shooting at him.

D) Goodnight's posterior inadvertently flips a switch that harnesses the power of the sun, aimed precisely at Bond's head.

319) TRUE or FALSE. As the book closes, Bond declines the offer of a knighthood because he "wants to remain a Scottish peasant."

320) Scaramanga had been raised in a circus and didn't find out that he enjoyed killing people until

A) someone shot his pet elephant.

B) his parents embarrassed him in public so he shot them both through the heart.

C) he was paid to kill someone's wife.

D) he shot the girl he was making love to during sex, because she had called him "Rodney" during her orgasm.

23 THAT'S WHY THEY CALL IT THE BOOB TUBE

321) On October 21, 1954, James Bond made his first live television appearance in a dramatic presentation. Who played the first Agent 007?
   A) Paul Newman
   B) Barry Nelson
   C) Robert Redford
   D) Cliff Robertson

322) In the late 1950s NBC was considering a show called "Commander Jamaica" as a potential dramatic adventure series. The main character was to be called James Gunn, and his base of operations was to be Morgan's Harbor, Jamaica. How is this related to James Bond?
   A) This show provided Ian Fleming with the inspiration to write a series of books about a character named James Bond, which he would also set in Jamaica.
   B) This show was created by Ian Fleming, but since it was never optioned he used the discarded story outlines as the basis for the collection entitled *FOR YOUR EYES ONLY.*
   C) This show was created by Fleming and it contained the story outline later used in his book *DOCTOR NO.*
   D) This show featured the very same story outline Fleming used in *LIVE AND LET DIE,* and resulted in a court case involving another author and Fleming.

323) Which Bond film received the highest audience share the first time it was broadcast on American television?
   A) *DOCTOR NO*
   B) *GOLDFINGER*
   C) *THUNDERBALL*
   D) *THE SPY WHO LOVED ME*

324) Home Box Office, America's largest pay-cable television service,
      usually shows the James Bond films in their original, uncut forms.
      What is the most popular Bond movie on HBO?
      A) *GOLDFINGER*
      B) *THE MAN WITH THE GOLDEN GUN*
      C) *THE SPY WHO LOVED ME*
      D) *FOR YOUR EYES ONLY*

325) In Great Britain, the home of Ian Fleming and Agent 007, the
      Bond movies are broadcast on the IBA (Independent Broadcast-
      ing Authority channels) around the nation. Of all the films aired
      so far, which has received the highest audience share (or TVR,
      as it's known in the U.K.)?
      A) *DOCTOR NO*
      B) *FROM RUSSIA WITH LOVE*
      C) *YOU ONLY LIVE TWICE*
      D) *THE SPY WHO LOVED ME*

326) Whom does Bond kill during the opening sequence on the snow-covered mountain?
   A) Martine Blanchard
   B) Sergei Borzov
   C) Agent Nikitin
   D) Agent Triple X

327) Where is 007 when "M" says to Miss Moneypenny, "Tell him to pull out. Immediately!"
   A) Austria
   B) Canada
   C) Italy
   D) Switzerland

328) When we first meet Anya, she's in bed with her Russian lover. Her phone rings, and we see that it's kept inside a music box. What is the music that plays on Anya's music box when she opens it?
   A) "Lara's Theme"
   B) "1812 Overture"
   C) "Nutcracker Suite"
   D) "The Internationale"

329) TRUE or FALSE. Anya gets the better of 007 by blowing sleep dust in his face while they argue outside the Temple of Karnak.

ROGER MOORE and BARBARA BACH

(CREDIT: CAMERON/SYGMA)

330) When James and Anya meet up at the Mojave Club, they saunter over to the bar and trade quips. Anya impresses Bond with her knowledge of his past by
   A) ordering the correct drink for him.
   B) saying that he was recruited from the Royal Navy.
   C) reminding him that his wife was killed.
   D) telling him his favorite dirty joke.

331) TRUE or FALSE. Ian Fleming claimed that he found the manuscript for *THE SPY WHO LOVED ME* on his desk one morning, and that, after clearing certain passages with the government so as not to violate the Official Secrets Act, he sponsored its publication.

332) _____ was the name of the location at Lake George, New York, where Vivienne Michel meets James Bond.
   A) Crescent Lake Motor Court
   B) Dreamy Pines Motor Court
   C) Glen Falls Ranch Cabins
   D) Loch Sheldrake Bungalow Colony

333) Pictured on the next page is the model for Stromberg's hideout in the movie, *THE SPY WHO LOVED ME.* What was it called?
   A) Atlantis
   B) Lipadus
   C) Liparus
   D) Xanadu

334) Where was this headquarters located?
   A) off the coast of Corsica
   B) off the coast of Majorca
   C) off the coast of Sardinia
   D) off the coast of Sicily

335) Bond pretends to be _____ when he arrives here to visit Stromberg.
   A) Robert Bruce, a clothing designer
   B) Robert Sterling, a marine biologist

121

(CREDIT: DON GRIFFIN, PERRY SUBMARINES)

The model for Stromberg's hideout

C) Robert Conrad, an underwater photographer
D) Robert Somerset, an author

336) In the novel, the two men who arrive at the motel to harass Vivienne were called
   A) Phancey and Sanguinetti.
   B) Sluggsy and Horror.
   C) Napolean and Illya.
   D) Morrow and O'Donnell.

337) Which of the following men do not become involved with Vivienne Michel?
   A) Derek Mallady
   B) Kurt Rainer
   C) Len Holbrook
   D) Horst Uhlman

338) What happens to Bond and Anya that forces them to drive off a dock and go under water?
   A) Jaws and a car filled with henchmen force them off the road, onto the dock and a presumed dead end.

B) A motorcycle sidecar chases them off the dock, exploding in midair behind them as they sink under the water.
C) Nothing forces them underwater. Bond purposely drives down there in order to get a closer look at Stromberg's place.
D) A pursuing helicopter keeps chase when all other thugs fail, and 007 has no choice but to take a dive in the drink.

339) When the car resurfaces on the beach, the beachgoers are, understandably, incredulous. There is one man in particular who assumes he's had far too much to drink, and does quite an effective double take. This man repeats this performance in two other films, but in this one, what is he drinking?
A) Cinzano
B) Martini & Rossi
C) Phillippe Rothschild
D) Bolla

340) When Anya learns that Bond was responsible for killing the man she loved, what does she vow to do?
A) give him a hickey he'll never forget
B) kill him the first chance she gets
C) kill him when the mission is over
D) make him very nervous, promising to kill him when he least expects it

Lotus Esprit and scuba diver underwater

(CREDIT: DON GRIFFIN, PERRY SUBMARINES)

341) Whom does Stromberg send to retrieve the plans for the radar tracking system?
   A) Jaws and Fekkesh
   B) Fekkesh and Kalba
   C) Kalba and Sandor
   D) Sandor and Jaws

342) TRUE or FALSE. Stromberg is interested in extortion, and will destroy New York and Moscow unless his demands are met by both Eastern and Western powers.

343) General Gogol's first name is mentioned while he and "M" converse inside the British Secret Service Pyramid Headquarters. What is his name?
   A) Alexis
   B) Joseph
   C) Leonid
   D) Ivan

344) As Bond tries to fashion his own bomb and fuse, he takes off an already existing fuse from a nuclear warhead. What must he be careful not to do?
   A) drop it
   B) let the conductor circuit touch the detonator
   C) let the detonator go off while it's still inside the bomb
   D) sneeze while holding the fuse

345) TRUE or FALSE. When the two-man sub containing Bond and Major Amasova reaches the waiting aircraft carrier, 007 and Anya are passionately making love. "M," "Q," Fred Grey, General Gogol and Admiral Hargreaves look on in utter amazement as the couple improve international relations.

25 IF YOU HUM A FEW BARS, I THINK I CAN FAKE IT

346) What is DOCTOR NO's calypso-style opening song?
   A) "Marianne"
   B) "The Belly Lick"
   C) "Three Blind Mice"
   D) "Underneath The Mango Tree"

347) In *MOONRAKER*, Bond follows a group of scientists into a special laboratory at the Venini Glass Works in Venice. In order to get inside the lab, a musical code must be played on the lock. What is the movie theme song that opens this electronic panel?
   A) theme from *CLOSE ENCOUNTERS OF THE THIRD KIND*
   B) theme from *GOLDFINGER*
   C) theme from *LAWRENCE OF ARABIA*
   D) the "James Bond" theme

348) In the opening titles of every Bond film, we generally are treated to beautiful women jumping, dancing, swinging, shooting and falling in various gymnastic positions. However, in one movie the singer of the title track actually appears on screen, singing the song throughout the credits. In which film does this occur?
   A) *FROM RUSSIA WITH LOVE*
   B) *THE MAN WITH THE GOLDEN GUN*
   C) *MOONRAKER*
   D) *FOR YOUR EYES ONLY*

349) In *THE SPY WHO LOVED ME*, every time Stromberg raises or lowers his sea-bound headquarters, a classical tune is played in the background. Name the song and the composer.
   A) Toccata and Fugue in D Minor by Johann Sebastian Bach
   B) Concerto no. 21 in C Major for Piano and Orchestra by Wolfgang Amadeus Mozart
   C) "Andante Cantible" from the Symphony No. 5 in E Minor by Peter Ilyitch Tchaikovsky

D) "Magic Fire Music" from *Die Walküre* by Richard Wagner

350) TRUE or FALSE. The "James Bond Theme" was written by Monty Norman.

351) Turn to page 127, and identify in order who these musical performers are. (HINT: They've all done a title track to a James Bond motion picture.)
   A) Herb Alpert, Englebert Humperdinck, Lulu
   B) Maynard Ferguson, Englebert Humperdinck, Rita Coolidge
   C) Herb Alpert, Tom Jones, Carly Simon
   D) Chuck Mangione, Tom Jones, Carly Simon

352) Now that you've successfully identified who these people are, match them up in order to the composers and lyricists who wrote their Bond theme songs.
   A) Burt Bacharach and Hal David, John Williams and Leslie Bricusse, Bill Conti and Michael Leeson
   B) John Barry and Don Black, Marvin Hamlisch and Carole Bayer Sager, John Barry and Hal David
   C) John Barry alone, Leslie Bricusse and Anthony Newley, Marvin Hamlisch and Carole Bayer Sager
   D) Burt Bacharach and Hal David, John Barry and Don Black, Marvin Hamlisch and Carole Bayer Sager

353) Match the singer with the song.
   A) Louis Armstrong   1) "All Time High"
   B) Shirley Bassey   2) "Do You Know How Christmas Trees Are Grown?"
   C) Rita Coolidge   3) "For Your Eyes Only"
   D) Sheena Easton   4) "From Russia With Love"
   E) Lani Hall   5) "Live And Let Die"
   F) Lulu   6) "The Look Of Love"

(COURTESY A & M RECORDS)

(COURTESY EPIC RECORDS)

(COURTEST WARNER BROS.
RECORDS)

G)	Paul McCartney and Wings	7)	"Make It Last All Night"
H)	Matt Munro	8)	"The Man With The Golden Gun"
I)	Nina	9)	"Moonraker"
J)	Rage	10)	"Never Say Never Again"
K)	Nancy Sinatra	11)	"You Only Live Twice"
L)	Dusty Springfield	12)	"We Have All The Time In The World"

354) Welsh-born singing star Shirley Bassey is connected to the Bond films for having sung how many title songs?

   A) 1
   B) 2
   C) 3
   D) 4

355) TRUE or FALSE. Considering all the talent behind the songs written for the James Bond films, it's remarkable that only one song ever won the Academy Award for "Best Original Song."

356) TRUE or FALSE. The entire action of the novel *MOONRAKER* takes place in Great Britain over the course of one five-day work week.

357) Gala Brand, an officer from Scotland Yard's Special Branch, works for Hugo Drax and is assigned to cooperate with James Bond when he arrives to replace a murdered agent. Although she is initially cool towards him, she does allow Bond to kiss her a few times. But 007 is never able to sleep with her. Why?
   A) because, like Pussy Galore and Rosa Klebb, she is a lesbian (or at least has leanings in that direction)
   B) because he never tries anything that bold with her
   C) because she's engaged to be married as soon as this mission is over
   D) because Gala Brand is a man

358) Who is Steffi Esposito?
   A) Drax's A.D.C., and the man responsible for killing Major Tallon
   B) the headwaiter at Blade's
   C) "M" 's butler
   D) the man who taught 007 how to cheat at cards

359) What must Bond do after Jaws tosses him out of the plane in the opening sequence?
   A) prepare to die
   B) grab onto one of the men with a parachute and hang on
   C) maneuver towards the lake and hope for the best
   D) steal a parachute from a steel-toothed man

360) Bond travels to visit Hugo Drax in his palatial estate pictured on the next page. This famous structure, known as the Vaux-le-Vicomte, is actually located near the French town of Fountainbleau. But to what American state is Drax supposed to have transported it "brick by brick"?

Vaux-le-Vicomte estate, France

(CREDIT: FRENCH GOV'T TOURIST OFFICE)

A) Arizona
B) California
C) Nevada
D) Texas

361) As Bond is helicoptered over the estate, Corrine Dufour points
out to 007 that Drax trains all of his hand-picked astronauts right
on his own grounds. Dressed in white and led by an instructor,
how many astronauts are seen doing calisthenics in front of the
estate?
A) 12
B) 18
C) 24
D) 36

362) Why is Great Britain involved in the space shuttle crisis?
A) The Moonraker was lost while on loan to the British.
B) The Moonraker contained a special satellite developed by
British Aerospace, the contents of which were highly classified.
C) The Moonraker was insured by Lloyd's of London, and
if the company was ever actually forced to pay, Britain's
economy would be rocked to its foundations.
D) The disappearance of the Moonraker struck fear in the
heart of every nation, so spies from all countries joined in
the search.

363) Corrine Clery played the helicopter pilot who delivered Bond
from the airport to Drax's estate. She also beds down with 007
on his very first night there, and then helps him to find Drax's
private safe. For her troubles
A) Bond asks her to marry him.
B) she's eaten to death by ferocious dobermans.
C) she's given the choice assignment as Miss Moneypenny's
new assistant (as we'll see when she reappears in *OCTO-
PUSSY*).
D) Jaws tosses her into the pool, where a 29-foot python

131

(CREDIT: GLOBE PHOTOS)

LOIS CHILES and ROGER MOORE

squeezes her to death. (Drax comments, "One good squeeze deserves another.")

364) When Bond first meets Dr. Holly Goodhead, pictured above, she offers to give him a tour of the entire facility. She puts Bond in the Centrifuge Trainer and shows him the "chicken switch" should the machine spin him around too quickly. At what speed does Bond have a flashback that reminds him of the wristwatch weapon he's wearing?
A) 3 g's
B) 7 g's
C) 13 g's
D) 18 g's

365) TRUE or FALSE. In the poster artwork advertising *MOON-RAKER,* Holly Goodhead wears the same tight-fitting white space outfit that she wears in the film during the space station scenes.

366) In Venice, Bernard Lee makes his last screen appearance as "M" in a James Bond motion picture. Bond has just embarrassed

Frederick Gray and "M" by barging in on an unassuming Hugo Drax. Before Gray and "M" return to London, what does 007's boss say?

A) "007, no slip ups, or we're both in trouble."
B) "That's another fine mess you've got us into."
C) "Keep me posted."
D) "You're off the case from this point on. Officially, that is."

367) In Rio, Bond and Holly team up again after their sudden separation in Venice. As they board the cable car that will descend Sugar Loaf Mountain (see the next page), what happens?

A) The car stops and Jaws arrives to try and kill 007.
B) They see one of Drax's planes leave the local airport.
C) Jaws climbs up the cable car wire, hand over hand, but falls when he reaches Bond's car.
D) They ride smoothly to the ground, undisturbed until Jaws appears at the cable car lift-off station.

368) What happens to Jaws after Bond and Holly disappear?

A) He takes a sip from a conveniently located bottle of "7-Up."
B) He meets a girl in pigtails as the love theme from "Romeo and Juliet" plays in the background.
C) He lifts a large steel wheel off his foot to free himself, but drops it rather unfortunately on a certain part of his anatomy.
D) He gets caught up in the reverie of a Brazilian "Junkanoo."

369) Why does Drax hire Zbigniew Krycsiwiki, otherwise known as Jaws?

A) He has a thing for men with steel teeth.
B) He needs a replacement for the deceased Chang.
C) He thinks someone familiar with Bond might have better luck eliminating him.
D) Jaws is looking for a job, and happens to be in South America at a propitious moment.

Cable car over Rio de Janiero

(CREDIT: BRAZILIAN TOURIST OFFICE)

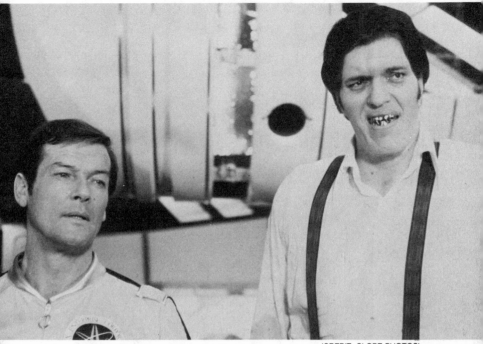

(CREDIT: GLOBE PHOTOS)

ROGER MOORE and RICHARD KIEL as "Jaws"

370) Bond kills the python in the pool outside Drax's Amazon headquarters with
    A)   an object he never knew was so sharp.
    B)   Holly's CIA-issue poison-tipped pen.
    C)   his bare hands, breaking its neck.
    D)   a large stick that he jabs into its throat.

371) When Jaws pulls 007 out of the water, he escorts a weary James
Bond to the space center control room. Perched over Drax's head
is a globe containing the deadly flower that helped wipe out an
entire race. That same flower has provided Drax with the chemi-
cals for his deadly poison. But how did the *orchidae negrum*
destroy a civilization?
    A)   Unaware of its poisonous capacity, the population unwit-
tingly used the flowers in preparing meals.
    B)   Unaware of its poisonous capacity, the population
smoked its dried leaves as a stimulant.
    C)   Unaware of its poisonous capacity, the population re-

ceived long-term exposure to its pollen and ultimately
became sterile.
- D) Everyone knew it was poisonous, but they harbored a
secret death wish.

372) In the novel, who was Loelia Ponsonby?
- A) Bond's private maid back in his Chelsea flat
- B) the secretary assigned to the "double O" section
- C) the name of the first woman in Bond's life
- D) the nickname given Bond's 1933 Bentley, an off-color
reference to some obscure English pornographic film
Fleming had once invested in

373) According to the novel, the Moonraker was
- A) an atomic rocket, a "gift" from Drax to Great Britain,
capable of hitting any target in Europe.
- B) a space shuttle program financed by Drax to propel the
British Space Program far ahead of its American counter-
part.
- C) the tallest mast on an old schooner, used as the symbol
for Drax's corporation (and ambitions).
- D) the name of Drax's palatial estate overlooking the English
Channel.

374) After six shuttles arrive at Drax's orbiting space station, Bond
and Holly are caught by Jaws and brought to Drax. But no sooner
does Jaws decide it's time to fight with rather than against 007
than the American space marines arrive. During the battle, how
does Drax meet his doom?
- A) He is choked to death by Jaws.
- B) He is laser-beamed by a space marine.
- C) He is ejected into outer space.
- D) He is crushed beneath a poisonous globe.

375) What is the last line in *MOONRAKER?*
- A) "I think he's attempting re-entry."
- B) "Just keeping the British end up, sir."
- C) "James, take me around the world one more time."
- D) "Why not?"

Moonraker Space Shuttle   (CREDIT: REVELL, INC.)

27 FAMOUS LAST WORDS

376) Who once said that "Bond is sadism for the family"?
   A) Sean Connery
   B) Pauline Kael
   C) Rex Reed
   D) Harry Saltzman

377) "Those who have read the books are likely to be disappointed, but those who haven't will find it a wonderful movie. Audiences laugh in all the right places." These words were spoken at the premiere of *DOCTOR NO* by
   A) Albert R. Broccoli
   B) Ian Fleming
   C) John F. Kennedy
   D) Terence Young

378) James Bond is asked by an adoring female what he does for a living. He replies, "I travel, sort of a licensed trouble-shooter." Who does he say this to?
   A) Honey Rider
   B) Patricia Fearing
   C) Jill Masterson
   D) Domino Vitali

379) Who said, "Good to see you, Mr. Bond. Things have been awfully dull around here . . . I hope we're going to have some gratuitous sex and violence."?
   A) A critic for the Chicago *Sun Times*
   B) Sheik Hosein in *THE SPY WHO LOVED ME*
   C) Algy in *NEVER SAY NEVER AGAIN*
   D) Q in *DIAMONDS ARE FOREVER*

380) "Of course, some critics might say that Bond is nothing more than an actor in the movies. But then, we've all got to start somewhere." Who said this?

A) President John F. Kennedy
B) Evita Peron
C) President Ronald Reagan
D) Charlton Heston

381) "We have all the time in the world"
A) was a reference Bond made to Felix Leiter inside Fort Knox while diffusing Goldfinger's atomic bomb.
B) is the name of a Fleming short story written while he was a reporter for the Sunday London *Times.*
C) was the last line uttered by Bond in *ON HER MAJESTY'S SECRET SERVICE.*
D) was how Drax felt after he released the deadly poison to contaminate the earth.

382) "This is no time to be rescued" is the last line of
A) *DOCTOR NO.*
B) *GOLDFINGER.*
C) *THUNDERBALL.*
D) *FOR YOUR EYES ONLY.*

383) In what film does crusty old "M" say, "What would I do without you, Miss Moneypenny? Thank you."
A) *ON HER MAJESTY'S SECRET SERVICE*
B) *DIAMONDS ARE FOREVER*
C) *LIVE AND LET DIE*
D) *THE MAN WITH THE GOLDEN GUN*

384) Who once described James Bond, Agent 007, as "An undercover agent in the British secret service, tough, hard-hitting, hard-drinking, hard-living and amoral, who at regular intervals saves the citizens of this country and the whole free world from the most incredible disasters"?
A) a film critic
B) a solicitor
C) a Baptist minister
D) a book critic

385) "It's a circus, I can't stop it now" was uttered by
  A) Cubby Broccoli.
  B) Charles K. Feldman.
  C) Kevin McClory.
  D) John Glen.

386) The movie version of *FOR YOUR EYES ONLY* is a hybrid of two short stories written by Ian Fleming. The first is obviously "For Your Eyes Only." What is the title of the other short story?
A) "James Bond in New York"
B) "Quantum of Solace"
C) "Risico"
D) "The Living Daylights"

387) The film begins as 007 pays his respects to his beloved wife Tracy at her cemetery plot in Stokes Poges Church, Buckinghamshire. According to the simple headstone, what year was Tracy born?
A) 1938
B) 1943
C) 1945
D) 1948

388) As Bond is taken for a ride through the Becton Gasworks in London's East End, a mysterious bald figure in a wheelchair controls his destiny. Although we know it's supposed to be Blofeld, his name is never mentioned, nor is it listed in the credits. But as 007 takes the crippled Blofeld by the chair and drops him into a tall smokestack, what does Blofeld helplessly shout?
A) "Mr. Bond, Mr. Bond . . . put me down."
B) "We can do a deal. I'll buy you a delicatessen made of stainless steel."
C) "I'll get you for this . . . and your little dog, too!"
D) "Bond, wait! I've a great recipe for pudding I can give you!"

389) Sir Timothy Havelock and his wife Iona are working in the Mediterranean for the British Government. After their daughter arrives, both are killed by a man circling in a plane overhead. Who kills the Havelocks?
A) Columbo
B) Gonzales

(CREDIT: SYGMA/PARIS)

C) Kristatos
D) Locque

390) Who plays the half-Greek, half-English marine biologist with a Ph.D. (pictured above) set to avenge the death of her parents?
   A) Jill Bennett
   B) Carole Bouquet
   C) Cassandra Harris
   D) Lynn-Holly Johnson

391) Bond and Melina are captured by Kristatos after they retrieve the *A.T.A.C.* from the *St. Georges.* Their death is supposed to be a painful one, in which they are tied up and dragged behind a boat along the sharp corals—the idea being that their blood will attract a school of hungry sharks. Although this was not in the Fleming short story of "For Your Eyes Only," it was the featured torture/death sequence in which other novel?
   A) *LIVE AND LET DIE*
   B) *THUNDERBALL*
   C) *THE HILDEBRAND RARITY*
   D) *OCTOPUSSY*

392) For some it's short, for others it's long. But on the head of the actress who played Melina Havelock, how long was it? (Her hair, that is.)

A) 14 inches
B) 26 inches
C) 38 inches
D) 40 inches

393) What does *A.T.A.C.* stand for?
   A) Advanced Telecom Audio Control
   B) Automatic Tracking Advance Communicator
   C) Automatic Travel Awareness Calculator
   D) Automatic Targeting Attack Communicator

394) According to the short story, Kristatos (played by Julian Glover —see the next page) works for the CIA as an informer, doing a little smuggling on the side as "extra cover." What does Kristatos want from 007 in order to help choke off the drug traffic to England?
   A) $30,000 and the death of the "Dove"
   B) 200,000 pounds and no questions asked regarding how he cuts off the drugs
   C) only the death of Enrico Colombo
   D) 200,000 pounds and the death of Enrico Colombo

395) With the death of Bernard Lee, the minister of defense and the chief of staff assumed the old admiral's duties for this movie. They tell Bond what has happened, assign him to the case and code name it
   A) Operation Undertoe.
   B) Operation Extase.
   C) Operation Recovery.
   D) Operation Crashdive.

396) Who kills Kristatos in the movie?
   A) James Bond
   B) Milos Columbo
   C) Melina Havelock
   D) Eric Kriegler

397) Many people try killing James Bond in this film. In fact, there are so many people interested in doing away with Jimmy that it's

JULIAN GLOVER

(CREDIT: RICHARD SCHENKMAN)

hard to distinguish the good guys from the bad guys. Of the following, who *didn't* work for Kristatos?
A) Apostis
B) Ferrara
C) Gonzales
D) Kriegler

398) As part of a promotion in *Playboy* magazine, a contest was held for some lucky contestant to win a role in *FOR YOUR EYES ONLY*. Which actress won that prize and made her motion picture debut in this film?
A) Toby Robins
B) Lalla Dean
C) Alison Worth
D) Robin Young

399) According to the Fleming short story, what was Lisl Baum's occupation?
A) croupier at the local casino
B) drug smuggler and paid assassin
C) personal whore
D) countess and aristocrat

400) Pictured on the next page is the Neptune, a two-man submarine used in the movie *FOR YOUR EYES ONLY*. How far under-

"The Neptune"

(CREDIT: DON GRIFFIN, PERRY SUBMARINES)

water do Bond and Melina take the sub, and what almost prevents them from returning to the surface alive?

- A) 584 feet, and another sub tries drilling a hole in their front window
- B) 550 feet, and a man wearing a "JIM" suit plants a limpet mine on the side of the Neptune
- C) 584 feet, and a man in the "JIM" suit cuts the electrical cables outside of the Neptune
- D) 550 feet, and another sub drops a thermite depth charge beneath the Neptune

401) TRUE or FALSE. During the *baccarat* game 007 plays in Corfu, Bond wins a hand when the croupier says he has a "9," even though he only shows a "5."

402) The part of Milos Colombo was
- A) played by a former "Tevye."
- B) played by a former television detective who makes a cameo appearance in *FOR YOUR EYES ONLY.*
- C) played by a man who appeared in the TV series "In Search of Alexander."
- D) the killer who worked for the Dove and was pushed over a cliff in his car by 007.

403) Our good friend General Gogol arrives from Moscow to collect the A.T.A.C. from Kristatos (see next page). Though he doesn't say a word (presumably this cost the producers less money), he does expect 007 to give him the device. What happens to the A.T.A.C.?
- A) Bond takes it back to England.
- B) Bond gives it to Gogol, waits for the Russian to take off and fly away, then switches on the self-destruct device attached to the A.T.A.C., blowing up the general and his helicopter.
- C) Columbo takes the A.T.A.C. back to Greece.
- D) Nobody takes the A.T.A.C. anywhere.

404) The original title of the short story "For Your Eyes Only" was

146

(CREDIT: JOHN BRYSON/SYGMA)

WALTER GOTELL, as General Gogol with Bond and henchman.

A) "Content Goes The Weasel."
B) "Death Goes On Holiday."
C) "For Your Eyes Only."
D) "Man's Work."

405) Bond is reluctant to kill in cold blood, but in the short story he accepts the assignment given to him by "M." What is this assignment?

A) to avenge the brutal murder of "M" 's personal friends
B) to seek out a drug smuggler and bring him to justice for selling drugs to a relative of the prime minister
C) to kill von Hammerstein for beating "M" at cards and winning close to 50,000 pounds
D) to retrieve a valuable communications device and cut off the steady flow of opium from one particular source

406) "Little Nellie" was
  A) the nickname for one of Blofeld's gay henchmen in *DIAMONDS ARE FOREVER.*
  B) the name of the mini autogiro in *YOU ONLY LIVE TWICE.*
  C) the young girl in *THE MAN WITH THE GOLDEN GUN* who pretended to be Bond's illegitimate daughter.
  D) the largest swamp alligator in *LIVE AND LET DIE;* the one that bit off Tee-Hee's arm, near New Orleans.

407) In which film does the character Jaws make his debut?
  A) *THUNDERBALL*
  B) *THE SPY WHO LOVED ME*
  C) *MOONRAKER*
  D) *OCTOPUSSY*

408) Which Bond film was inspired by a real-life adventure involving the late and reclusive mega-billionaire, Howard Hughes?
  A) *DIAMONDS ARE FOREVER*
  B) *THE MAN WITH THE GOLDEN GUN*
  C) *THE SPY WHO LOVED ME*
  D) *NEVER SAY NEVER AGAIN*

409) TRUE or FALSE. *DOCTOR NO* is the only Ian Fleming James Bond novel ever to be legally published within the Soviet Union.

410) How is *OCTOPUSSY* executive producer and writer Michael G. Wilson related to Cubby Broccoli?
  A) He's his son.
  B) He's his grandson.
  C) He's his stepson.
  D) He's his nephew.

411) TRUE or FALSE. Since 1975 when co-producer Harry Saltzman sold out his interest in Eon Productions, Cubby Broccoli and

United Artists have co-produced the James Bond movies with Columbia Pictures.

412) Even though we only know him as "Q," the character played by Desmond Llewelyn has an actual name. What is it?
   A)   Major Benz
   B)   Major Boothroyd
   C)   Major Haydon
   D)   Major Vallance

413) A total of ten Academy Award nominations have been bestowed on the first 13 James Bond movies released. How many Oscars has "JB" won?
   A)   0
   B)   1
   C)   2
   D)   5

414) James Bond plays *chemin de fer* in many of the novels and films. Haven't you learned the rules by now? For instance, how many decks of cards are there in a shoe?
   A)   two
   B)   six
   C)   ten
   D)   An unlimited supply keeps flowing in from the croupier.

415) In which film did Sean Connery's first wife, Diane Cilento, don a black wig and substitute during the shooting of underwater scenes for an actress suffering from heat prostration?
   A)   *DOCTOR NO*
   B)   *THUNDERBALL*
   C)   *YOU ONLY LIVE TWICE*
   D)   *DIAMONDS ARE FOREVER*

416) The rocket-firing, two-man submarine pictured on the next page is called the Shark Hunter II and is fully functional. In what picture was it used?

The "Shark Hunter II" underwater

A) *THUNDERBALL*
B) *THE SPY WHO LOVED ME*
C) *FOR YOUR EYES ONLY*
D) All of the above

417) The name of a character that appears in *GOLDFINGER* is also the name of a television character created by Ian Fleming before his James Bond movies became popular. What is that name?
A) Dancer
B) Drake
C) Smiley
D) Solo

418) TRUE or FALSE. The James Bond 007 Fan Club, started in 1974, has members in over 20 countries and has grown to become a major industry, with large offices and a staff of approximately 20.

419) What is "Bondage"?
A) the name of a magazine
B) a sexual technique preferred by 007
C) the annual New Orleans James Bond convention
D) a code word meaning, roughly, how old a certain Bond character really is

420) We know that Doctor No has a stolen painting on display in his private abode. But in what other James Bond film, written by one of the authors of *DOCTOR NO,* do we find another stolen art object on display in someone's home?
   A) *GOLDFINGER*
   B) *CASINO ROYALE*
   C) *THE MAN WITH THE GOLDEN GUN*
   D) *OCTOPUSSY*

421) "Octopussy" was published in the United States two years after the death of Ian Fleming. In this short story, James Bond is sent from London to a place called Wavelets, where he interviews a man called Major Dexter Smythe. Why is Bond sent?
    A) He's looking for information regarding the whereabouts of a cache of World War II gold bars.
    B) He's looking for information regarding the death of Herr Oberhauser during World War II.
    C) He wants Smythe to return the weapons he has stolen from the British Secret Service.
    D) He wants to convince Smythe to continue his experiments dealing with underwater colonization back in England.

422) What happens to Smythe?
    A) He returns to England with Bond.
    B) He is killed by his pet "octopussy" after being stung by a poisonous fish.
    C) He marries Mary Parnell, raises a daughter and lives quietly with his inner turmoil.
    D) He drowns himself the next day.

423) The movie of *OCTOPUSSY,* as does *FOR YOUR EYES ONLY,* draws upon two Ian Fleming short stories for its content. What story aside from "Octopussy" contributed to the movie?
    A) "The Hildebrand Rarity"
    B) "The Living Daylights"
    C) "The Property of a Lady"
    D) "Quantum of Solace"

424) In an obscure Latin American country, Bond is delivered to a horse show by the lovely agent, Bianca. After Bond is arrested for impersonating a colonel, Bianca distracts the male guards aboard a transport truck, allowing 007 the opportunity to jump free and sneak into her horse trailer. Who plays Bianca?

Jeep, horse-box and AcroJet, Corgi Toys   (CREDIT: REEVES INTERNATIONAL)

A) Louise King
B) Tina Hudson
C) Eva Rueber-Staier
D) Alison Worth

425) When 007 takes off in the AcroJet (pictured above), he's flying in what is considered the world's smallest jet. Only two of them are in existence today, each 12' long and 5'8" high. In the film, who did the actual piloting of the plane?
A) Corkey Fornof
B) Roger Moore
C) Bob Simmons
D) It was operated by remote control in case anything went wrong.

426) 009 turns up in West Berlin, wearing a clown suit, and a dagger in his back. But he's carrying a priceless Coronation Egg created by Carl Fabergé. Who was this egg originally created for?

(COURTESY OF ARTIST)

    A)   General Orlov
    B)   Tsar Peter the Great
    C)   Tsar Nicholas I
    D)   Tsar Nicholas II

427) At Sotheby's, 007 and art expert Jim Fanning participate in an auction for the egg. When the price reaches _____ , Bond switches the real egg with a fake one.
    A)   400,000 pounds
    B)   425,000 pounds
    C)   450,000 pounds
    D)   500,000 pounds

428) Two people attending the auction become of particular interest to 007. One is Kamal Khan, played by Louis Jourdan, and the other is (refer to above photo)
    A)   Magda, played by Kirstin Wainwright.
    B)   Magda, played by Kristina Wayborn.
    C)   Maggie, played by Kristina Wayble.
    D)   Mufit, played by Kirstin Wayborn.

429) In India, Bond and Magda retire to 007's bedroom. After he notices her little "octopussy" (a tatoo on her back), Bond allows Magda to escape with the Fabergé Egg. Why?

154

A) It is in payment for his delightful evening.
B) He doesn't see her take it.
C) She promises that she'll return it as soon as possible.
D) He hopes it will lead him to 009's killers.

430) Bond arrives in Udaipur, India, and is greeted by Vijay, an agent working with the British. What is he doing when they first meet?
A) Vijay is selling snake oil out of a suitcase.
B) Vijay is charming a snake with the "James Bond" theme.
C) Vijay is charming a snake with a sharp stick and a hoop.
D) Vijay is showing some small children how to play tennis.

431) Who resides in the Monsoon Palace?
A) General Orlov
B) Gobinda and Toro
C) Octopussy and her girls
D) Kamal Khan

432) Even though Kamal Khan is currently living in India, we know he's an exiled prince. From what country is he exiled?
A) Afghanistan
B) Bhutan
C) Nepal
D) Pakistan

433) Kamal Khan invites Bond to dinner. He tells 007 that unless he talks,
A) he'll be tortured with Beethoven and war films for a fortnight.
B) he'll suffer permanent brain damage from curare injections.
C) he'll suffer permanent nerve damage from pentathol injections.
D) he'll suffer permanent space sickness from quadrotriticale.

434) What name does "M" give the assignment that sends Bond to India?

(CREDIT: JOHN BRYSON/SYGMA)

Louis Jourdan riding atop an elephant in sedan

    A) Operation Corona
    B) Operation Eggs
    C) Operation Punjab
    D) Operation Trove

435) During the course of *OCTOPUSSY,* Bond kills quite a number of swarthy individuals. Whom does he kill to avenge the death of 009?
    A) Gobinda
    B) Khan
    C) Twin Number One
    D) Twin Number Two

436) General Orlov wants an atomic bomb to be detonated in the West because
    A) he's always hated German food.
    B) he wants to help the disarmament movement.
    C) he wants to conquer the free world.
    D) he wants to show the old-fashioned Russian gerontocracy how to wage war in the 1980s.

437) Why doesn't Octopussy (Maud Adams) kill James Bond when they meet?

A) She doesn't know his real identity.

B) She wants to go to bed with him.

C) She wants to thank him for allowing her father to die honorably.

D) She tries to have him killed, but 007's too foxy.

438) Maud Adams is the first female personality to make a reappearance in a starring role in a James Bond film. When she first appeared in *THE MAN WITH THE GOLDEN GUN,* she played

A) Andrea Anderson, Scaramanga's errand girl.

B) Andrea Anders, Scaramanga's concubine.

C) Mary Goodnight, James Bond's assistant.

D) Mary MacGregor, secretary to the "double 0" section.

439) Octopussy's International Circus arrives for a performance in Feldstadt, West Germany. During the performance, we see all kinds of circus acts. What is the name of the "human cannonball"?

A) Giovanni the Great

B) Francisco the Fearless

C) Fearless Fosdick

D) The Flying Credenzas

440) Before Kamal Khan leaves India, he takes with him printing plates to make counterfeit money. What currency doesn't he have a plate for?

A) American dollars

B) French francs

C) German marks

D) Japanese yen

31 YOU'RE GOING OUT THERE A NOBODY, BUT YOU'RE COMING BACK A STAR . . .

441) TRUE or FALSE. Sean Connery is older than Roger Moore.

442) What does actress Lana Turner have in common with Cubby Broccoli, Sean Connery and Roger Moore?
   A) nothing
   B) They all went to the same grammar school.
   C) They all made a picture together.
   D) They all worked with her at least once in their careers.

443) In an interview in *Life* magazine, Sean Connery said that he'd like to give up acting and
   A) sail around the world.
   B) open a chain of fish restaurants.
   C) become a farmer.
   D) do absolutely nothing.

444) Which other James Bond family regular went to the Royal Academy of Dramatic Arts with Roger Moore?
   A) Bernard Lee
   B) Desmond Llewellyn
   C) Lois Maxwell
   D) Bob Simmons

445) After deciding he'd had enough of Bond, Sean Connery retired after *YOU ONLY LIVE TWICE.* Before the producers selected Australian model George Lazenby to play 007 for *ON HER MAJESTY'S SECRET SERVICE,* whom did they almost sign?
   A) Richard Burton
   B) Adam West (TV's "Batman")
   C) Lee Marvin
   D) John Gavin

446) A Broadway choreographer and the spokesperson for a famous carbonated beverage appeared as a laughing and dancing villain in

A) *GOLDFINGER*
B) *LIVE AND LET DIE*
C) *FOR YOUR EYES ONLY*
D) *OCTOPUSSY*

447) One actor in a Bond movie was dying, and worked despite tremendous pain throughout the assignment. Although he eventually took his own life, he worked on the film in order to leave his family more money. The actor was
A) Pedro Armendariz
B) Curt Jurgens
C) Bernard Lee
D) Robert Shaw

448) In what film does Sean Connery sing?
A) *DOCTOR NO*
B) *THUNDERBALL*
C) *YOU ONLY LIVE TWICE*
D) *DIAMONDS ARE FOREVER*

449) TRUE or FALSE. Connery has two tatoos on his right arm. One says, "Mum and Dad," the other, "Scotland Forever."

450) Of the following titles, what was the name of a show that did *not* star Roger Moore?
A) "Ivanhoe"
B) "The Saint"
C) "Maverick"
D) "Bat Masterson"

451) Executive Producer Kevin McClory owned the rights to produce a James Bond film of his own because he
   A) bought the rights to *THUNDERBALL* before Eon Productions did.
   B) co-authored the original *THUNDERBALL* story with Fleming.
   C) was given the rights by Eon Productions after their successful collaboration on *THUNDERBALL*.
   D) was a shrewd businessman who talked Eon Productions out of the rights to *THUNDERBALL* in 1959.

452) After all this time, why did Sean Connery agree to return to the role that made him famous?
   A) He thought it would be interesting.
   B) He needed the money.
   C) He lost a card game to Jack Schwartzman.
   D) He was no longer afraid of being typed as 007.

453) SPECTRE makes its first reappearance in a James Bond movie since *DIAMONDS ARE FOREVER*, back in 1971. When was SPECTRE "born"?
   A) in the movie *DOCTOR NO*
   B) in the book *DOCTOR NO*
   C) in the book *CASINO ROYALE*
   D) in the script for *THUNDERBALL*

454) Where does Bond first meet Fatima Blush?
   A) at Shrublands, where he oversees her assisting Captain Jack Petachi
   B) at the docks in Nassau while he's searching for the atomic weapons
   C) at the docks in Nassau, where she's just finished water skiing and he's just ordered a martini
   D) at Largo's charity ball

BARBARA CARRERA as
Fatima Blush

(CREDIT: DAVID STEEN/SYGMA)

455) What must Fatima do before she kills a man?
  A) her nails
  B) purchase a large snake
  C) hurt his feelings
  D) make love to him

456) Fatima is a victim of her own vanity. She's good at what she does (in every respect), and wants the world to know it. But her vanity is her downfall. How so?
  A) She wants 007 to admit she's a better lover than one of her predecessors—a girl he met in Philadelphia.
  B) She's caught doing her hair when Bond shoots her with his lasar wristwatch.
  C) She gets into a wrestling match with Domino, who accidentally kills her with a diamond stick-pin.
  D) As she gazes at her reflection, Largo's special two-way mirror explodes in her face.

457) Who plays "Q," the armorer in *NEVER SAY NEVER AGAIN*?
  A) Klaus Maria Brandauer, as Ambrose
  B) Edward Fox, as Algernon
  C) Rowan Atkinson, as Ambrose
  D) Alec McCowen, as Algernon

458) In order for Pettachi to steal the nuclear weapons, he must be able to duplicate the President of the United States' "eye print." How

much time does he have to convince the machine that his right eye is really the President's?

- A) 3 seconds
- B) 8 seconds
- C) 10 seconds
- D) 30 seconds

459) TRUE or FALSE. When SPECTRE issues its demands, the Western powers have seven days in which to turn over 25 billion dollars worth of uncut diamonds at a specified location. This plot device is also used in the original novel of *THUNDERBALL.*

460) Bond arrives at the famous Casino in Monte Carlo. What doesn't happen inside?

- A) He doesn't dance with Domino.
- B) He doesn't play a video game.
- C) He doesn't subdue a guard with a cigarette case.
- D) He doesn't win at *baccarat.*

Monte Carlo Casino

461) TRUE or FALSE. During production, real croupiers were hired to watch over the thousands of fake thousand-franc chips used at each of the gambling tables.

462) Maximilian Largo challenges Bond to a holographic video game which starts off amicably, but soon degenerates into a tense battle of wills. As they play for the rights to the world, what country is not individually played for?
   A) Japan
   B) France
   C) Spain
   D) The United States of America

463) SPECTRE hijacks two nuclear weapons and plans to hold the world at ransom. What is the name given to this operation?
   A) Operation Thunderball
   B) Operation Palmyra
   C) Operation Tears of Allah
   D) Operation Wells of Allah

464) Why doesn't 007 die when he's stabbed during the opening sequence?
   A) The attack on the Latin village is fake.
   B) The attacker unwittingly stabs 007's wallet.
   C) James Bond isn't really in this sequence: the man is a double (as in the murder scene with Grant in *FROM RUSSIA WITH LOVE*).
   D) Bond's famous gun-metal cigarette case saves him.

465) In the movie, the name of Largo's luxurious yacht is
   A) the *Nabila.*
   B) the *Disco Volante.*
   C) the *Flying Saucer.*
   D) the *Gravitar.*

466) At Shrublands, Bond gets into a brawl with Lippe. What kills this SPECTRE agent?

(CREDIT: WIDE WORLD PHOTOS)

SEAN CONNERY and KIM BASINGER as Domino on horseback

    A)   the food in the kitchen
    B)   Bond's urine specimen
    C)   a set of weights
    D)   a test tube

467)   Sean Connery introduces himself to Domino with the immortal words "My name is Bond, James Bond." Where is he as he speaks?
    A)   at the health spa in Nice
    B)   at the casino in Monte Carlo
    C)   aboard Largo's ship in the dance room
    D)   on the floor doing the tango

468)   *NEVER SAY NEVER AGAIN* is based on the same material that spawned the novel and movie *THUNDERBALL.* But what happens in *NEVER SAY NEVER AGAIN* that doesn't reach the screen in *THUNDERBALL?*

A) Domino saves Bond's life by killing Largo underwater.

B) Bond arrives at Shrublands with his Bentley.

C) Domino orders a Bloody Mary when Bond orders his vodka.

D) All of the above.

469) TRUE or FALSE. Although Sean Connery dances a mean tango with Domino, the former "Mr. Scotland" has never before been paid to dance in public.

470) *NEVER SAY NEVER AGAIN* contains some of the most beautiful women ever assembled for a movie. Match the actress with the part.

A)	Barbara Carrera	1)	Nicole
B)	Kim Basinger	2)	Lady in the Bahamas
C)	Prunella Gee	3)	Fatima Blush
D)	Saskia Cohen Tanui	4)	Miss Moneypenny
E)	Valerie Leon	5)	Domino
F)	Pamela Salem	6)	Patricia

33 EXTRA ADDED BONDAGE

471) In his collection *THRILLING CITIES,* Ian Fleming included a
short story entitled "James Bond in New York." In it, Agent 007
travels to New York City in order to
   A) personally return a special decoding device which the
   United States had loaned to the British.
   B) warn a former Secret Service officer that she was now
   living with an active KGB agent attached to the United
   Nations.
   C) interrogate a pair of Bulgarians on behalf of Ronald Val-
   lance of Scotland Yard.
   D) avenge the deaths of two of "M" 's old naval buddies.

472) Where was Bond supposed to make contact with Solange?
   A) at Scribner's, where there was a salesman who had a good
   "nose for thrillers"
   B) at the Carlyle Hotel, the "last great hotel in New York"
   C) at the Reptile House in the Central Park Zoo
   D) at the front gates of the Dakota apartment complex

473) "From a View to a Kill" was a short story included in the
collection *FOR YOUR EYES ONLY.* When the story opens,
James Bond is in Paris after a failed mission along the Austro-
Hungarian border. As he drinks, he reminisces about what hap-
pened to him when he first came to Paris at the age of sixteen.
What happened to him back then?
   A) He learned that his parents had both been killed.
   B) He lost his virginity and his wallet in a bar.
   C) He lost all his money in a card game with a Roumanian
   card sharp ("who knew more tricks than Houdini").
   D) He fell in love and bought his first Bentley.

474) Mary Ann Russell
   A) worked for Station "P" and found 007 drinking in Harry's
   bar.
   B) saved Bond's life with a .22 pistol.

C) was the name of the girl Bond always visited while in Paris.

D) was the maiden name of Bond's mother.

475) "The Hildebrand Rarity" first appeared in *Playboy* magazine in 1960. What was "the Hildebrand Rarity"?

A) a special ruby found in a particularly trecherous jungle

B) a rare flower found on a remote island near the Seychelles

C) a unique member of the squirrelfish family

D) a scientific phenomenon dealing with theoretically "clean" nuclear explosions

476) How does Milton Krest meet his timely demise?

A) He's thrown overboard by an angry sailor.

B) He's lost at sea during an angry storm.

C) His throat is cut by an angry passenger.

D) A large fish is stuffed down his throat.

477) In "Risico," Bond is sent by "M" to _____ to find the major source of drug smuggling into England.

A) France

B) Italy

C) Greece

D) Turkey

478) "Quantum of Solace" is, generously speaking, a long-winded story that features James Bond simply as "a listener." But we do learn a little bit about 007 himself. He says that if he should ever get married (this is before Fleming wrote *ON HER MAJESTY'S SECRET SERVICE*), he'll

A) have to be too old to do much else.

B) marry either an airline stewardess or a Japanese girl.

C) marry either someone incredibly rich or someone incredibly smart.

D) have his head examined by the best specialists.

479) "The Living Daylights" first appeared in *Argosy* magazine in 1962. In it, 007 is sent to Berlin in order to help a British agent

sneak back into the West. But why does this mission turn out to be a failure?

A) Bond did not kill a certain Russian sniper.

B) The agent coming to the West had been killed at the Berlin Wall.

C) The NKVD officers took cyanide rather than let Bond take them to London.

D) George Smiley took over at the last minute, leaving Bond out in the cold when Karla crossed the border.

480) "The Property of a Lady" was Fleming's last short story commissioned by Sotheby's. In the story, Maria Freudenstein was

A) the "janitor" who kept the "safe house" near Sotheby's fully stocked with Stolichnaya and black bread.

B) the name of the Fabergé egg being auctioned off.

C) the woman who took Bond to the auction in order to try and spot the KGB control in London.

D) the mole in the Secret Service who was feeding information to the Russians.

481) After the publication of his seventh novel, *GOLDFINGER*, Ian Fleming found his creation the subject of widespread satire and imitation. Among the more notorious rip-offs of 007 was a story, written by two Harvard undergraduates, called "Alligator." It was about

A) a man who painted people purple, kidnapped the Queen of England and tried to send the Houses of Parliament floating down the Thames River.

B) the founder of Izod-Lacoste and the origin of the famous shirt logo. "Mr. Gator" and a fellow named J***S B**D are engaged in a duel to the death.

C) a black gangster with a fetish for fine shoes and handbags, who corners the market on imported wallets, sending 007 into action on behalf of British industry.

D) a SPECTRE-like organization that used the London Underground as a warehouse for nuclear weapons and a way to get beneath the Tower of London in order to steal the Crown Jewels.

482) In "Colonel Sun," a James Bond story written by "Robert Markham," 007 follows a trail leading to Greece where he tries to rescue a kidnapped "M." After averting an international crisis, he is offered perhaps the oddest award of his career. What is it?
A) the Ramon Magsaysay Award for International Understanding
B) the Order of the Red Banner
C) the Companion of the Order of St. Michael and St. George
D) the Lenin Peace Prize

483) In 1973, Fleming's biographer John Pearson wrote *JAMES BOND—THE AUTHORIZED BIOGRAPHY OF 007.* Among the multitude of interesting facts offered is that Bond lost his virginity to a girl named Alys, that the owner of a brothel was his first true love, and
A) that he was engaged to be married to a woman named Muriel at the age of 21.
B) that Bond actually met Ian Fleming during a ski trip to Kitzbuhel.
C) that Bond's flat in Chelsea was located at No. 30 Wellington Square.
D) all of the above
E) none of the above

484) In 1977, Christopher Wood wrote a new novelization based on his screenplay for *THE SPY WHO LOVED ME.* Of the following, what happens in the book that doesn't happen in the movie?
A) Bond is beaten silly at the Pyramids by Anya's thugs.
B) Bond makes love to the woman at Fekkesh's house.
C) Bond is taken away by the Russians to a torture house where his genitals are connected to a large battery.
D) all of the above
E) none of the above

485) Christopher Wood wrote another James Bond novelization in 1979, this one based on his screenplay for *MOONRAKER*. In it, a large variety of ladies make passes at Her Majesty's most famous spy. But who actually goes to bed with him?
   A) Corrine Dufour, Holly Goodhead and Manuela
   B) Corrine Dufour and Holly Goodhead
   C) Trudi Parker, Corrine Dufour, Holly Goodhead and Manuela
   D) Trudi Parker, Holly Goodhead and Manuela

486) By 1980, John Gardner had assumed the Fleming mantle and began writing new James Bond novels that would carry the ageless superspy into the 1980s. Beginning with *LICENSE RENEWED* in 1981, what kind of car does 007 drive?
   A) a Mark II Continental
   B) a Lotus Turbo
   C) a Saab 900
   D) a Volvo 1200

487) Why does Bond steal Lavender Peacock's priceless necklace when he first sees her at Ascot?
   A) For the money—he's had it with the Secret Service, wants to "go private," settle down with "Q'ute" from "Q" branch, but he needs the money to do it right.
   B) So he can scream bloody murder, causing enough chaos to give him the chance to hide a homing device in Anton Murik's car.
   C) So he can appear to discover them, look like a nice guy and hopefully charm his way into getting an invitation to visit Lavender and Anton at Murik Castle.
   D) So he can return them to Sotheby's in London, from whence they were stolen.

488) In *FOR SPECIAL SERVICES,* James Bond teams up with Cedar Leiter, daughter of his old pal Felix. When Cedar and Bond arrive at the Rancho Bismaquer to check out Markus Bismaquer and his wife, Nena, they are given separate cabins. But

on the first night there, Cedar goes into her cabin and screams
when she sees
A) the decapitated head of a python snake.
B) Markus Bismaquer and Walter Luxor *in flagrante delicto.*
C) her bed covered with harvester ants.
D) Mike Maddox aiming his Colt .45 at her.

489) In *ICEBREAKER,* everyone who works with James Bond seems
to be or have been, at one time or another, a double or triple
agent. By the end of the story, when everything is explained to
us, who turns out to be "the good guys"?
A) Kolya Mosolov and Paula Vacker
B) Paula Vacker and Bad Brad Tirpitz
C) Rivke Ingber and Count Konrad von Gloda
D) Rivke Ingber and Kolya Mosolov

490) In all of John Gardner's James Bond novels, why is it odd that
James Bond is still referred to as "007"?
A) The "double O" section had been phased out in the mid-
1970s.
B) No one outside the British Secret Service, the USA and
other friendly services knew that was Bond's number.
C) Bond was no longer a member of the "double O" section,
having been forced out by age requirements.
D) It wasn't odd at all, that was his number and he was from
that section of Secret Service.

QUESTIONNAIRE

491) In what country was James Bond born?
   A) England
   B) Scotland
   C) Germany
   D) Switzerland

492) What is James Bond's birthday?
   A) October 11, 1920
   B) October 11, 1930
   C) November 11, 1920
   D) November 11, 1930

493) What were Bond's parents' names?
   A) Andrew Bond and Monique Dellacroix
   B) Andrew Bond and Monica Dellahoya
   C) James Bond and Mona Dellacroix
   D) Peter Bond and Monique D'Allesandro

494) How did Bond's parents die?
   A) in a plane crash
   B) in a climbing accident
   C) in a shipwreck
   D) They were lost on safari.

495) Who raised the orphaned James Bond, and in what town?
   A) Aunt Charlene in Mayfair
   B) Aunt Charmain in Pett Bottom
   C) Aunt Cheryl in Blackpool
   D) Uncle Charlie in Glasgow

496) What is Bond's official title?
   A) Commander James Bond, C.M.G., R.N.V.R.
   B) Sir James Bond, C.M.G., R.N.V.R.

C) Commander James Bond, C.M.G., R.N.V.R. (Ret.)

D) Lieutenant Commander James Bond, C.M.G., R.N.V.R.

497) TRUE or FALSE. James Bond is not a father.

498) As a principal officer in the Civil Service, James Bond
   A) received 1,500 pounds a year salary, with an expense account for the time he was on assignment.
   B) was entitled to a pension when he retired at the mandatory age of 45.
   C) generally received two major assignments each year, with the rest of his time devoted to paperwork.
   D) took no official holidays (or vacations), but was usually given leave by "M" after particularly tough assignments.

499) In all of the Ian Fleming *stories,* how many people has James Bond killed?
   A) 44 men and no women (though he was the indirect cause of the death of 4 women)
   B) 478 men and women, including all those who died at Crab Key and Fort Knox
   C) 21 men and no women
   D) 42 men and one woman

500) In the 13 movies produced by Eon Productions, how many people has James Bond personally killed (either with a gun, knife, object or strangulation)?
   A) 58
   B) 86
   C) 130
   D) 196

THE ANSWERS

IN THE BEGINNING . . .

1) **D.**

Fleming has said in several interviews that he started writing *CASINO ROYALE* "because my mental hands were empty and as a counter-irritant, or antibody, to my hysterical alarm at getting married at the age of 43." The novel was started ten weeks before his wedding day, and he finished the last sentence of the first draft six days before exchanging vows with his new bride.

2) **B.**

At first, Fleming's conception of the character called for a dull and uninteresting man to whom exciting things happened. He wanted the name to be just as dull, and so "borrowed" the name "James Bond" from the author of *BIRDS OF THE WEST INDIES,* one of his favorite books. "(I thought) my God, that's the dullest name I've ever heard, so I appropriated it. Now the dullest name in the world has become an exciting one. Mrs. Bond once wrote me a letter thanking me for using it."

3) **C.**

Whitehall used the "double 0" to classify top-secret documents during World War II, and Fleming was closely involved with the British intelligence effort during the war.

4) **B.**

It's located in the village of Oracabessa, and Fleming bought it in 1945, and was later to use it for his annual "escape" from London. Each of his Bond novels and short stories was written there, either in whole or in part. The name itself was taken either from Carson McCuller's novel *Reflections in a*

Golden Eye, or from the World War II operation "Goldeneye," since Fleming himself has mentioned both as the origin of this name.

5) **C.**

Even before *CASINO ROYALE* had been published, Fleming bought up this small company for tax purposes (in case he got rich off of Bond). Later, when his success was greater than he had ever imagined, he had to sell 51 percent of Glidrose and turn it into a public concern. So, in March of 1964, Booker Brothers, McConnell and Company paid 100,000 pounds to acquire a controlling interest in the company. Booker Brothers' chief interests at the time were sugar, rum and insurance, and to this day they run Glidrose. Booker Brothers owns the serialization and literary rights (through Glidrose) for all of Fleming's works, but the film and television rights are controlled by other people.

6) **TRUE.**

While at first reluctant to see his character treated as a subject for a daily comic strip, Fleming eventually gave in when he was assured of the quality of the work. In the spring of 1957, the London *Daily Express* ran the comic strip version of *CASINO ROYALE,* which was soon followed by comic strips of *LIVE AND LET DIE, DIAMONDS ARE FOREVER, FROM RUSSIA WITH LOVE, DOCTOR NO, GOLDFINGER, FROM A VIEW TO A KILL, FOR YOUR EYES ONLY, ON HER MAJESTY'S SECRET SERVICE* and *YOU ONLY LIVE TWICE.* In the 1960s, new adventures were written for the superspy, but shortly afterwards the strip stopped running. *THE ILLUSTRATED JAMES BOND, 007* is a collection of three full-length strips *(DIAMONDS ARE FOREVER, FROM RUSSIA WITH LOVE, DOCTOR NO)* and is published by the James Bond 007 Fan Club in Bronxville, New York.

7) **B.**

The wedding was held in the Town Hall, and Noel Coward and Cole Lesley (Coward's biographer) were the witnesses. A smiling, toothless black man entertained the attendants with this extremely off-color calypso song, and Fleming later had 007 insist that a native girl sing the blue words during the party held for Scaramanga's friends in chapter 10 of *THE MAN WITH THE GOLDEN GUN.*

8) **FALSE.**

The J.F.K. favorite was *FROM RUSSIA WITH LOVE,* which was among ten titles listed by candidate Kennedy as favorite books. Fleming met President Kennedy a few times; he was initially introduced to him by his friend

Mrs. Marion Leiter (undoubtedly the source of the name given to Fleming's CIA literary creation).

9) **B.**

Fleming knew Niven and had always pictured this suave and urbane gentleman as the perfect actor to play Bond.

10) **D.**

Twelve full-length novels (including *THE SPY WHO LOVED ME*) and nine short stories (including "James Bond in New York," a small piece included in his book *THRILLING CITIES*).

THE NAME'S THE THING

11) **A–9, B–2, C–6, D–1, E–3, F–5, G–4, H–7, I–8, J–10.**

Simone Latrelle was also known as Solitaire, and Dominetta Vitali was called Domino.

12) **TRUE.**

But only in the book: In the film version of *DIAMONDS ARE FOREVER,* Tiffany was supposed to have received her name because she was born on the first floor of the famous store while her mother shopped for a wedding ring.

13) **D.**

Another name listed outside Universal Exports was "Delaney Bros. (1944) Ltd." The novel *MOONRAKER* tells us that Miss Twinning was a real person who sat at the front entrance and politely brushed off people who wanted to have their radios checked or something exported.

14) **A–5, B–7, C–3 or 6, D–3 or 6, E–1, F–2, G–8 or 9, H–4, I–10, J–8 or 9.**

"Frank Westmacott" was the name on Bond's passport when he resurfaced after he had been missing for over a year. "Mark Hazard," while a cover identity for James Bond, was actually a field representative for "Transworld Consortium," the new name for the old "Universal Export."

15) **FALSE.**

When Fleming first created SPECTRE, that's what he thought it might stand for. But today and forever, SPECTRE stands for "(The) Special

Executive for Counter-intelligence, Terrorism, Revenge and Extortion," an organization not to be toyed with (unless, of course, you're James Bond).

THE MEN WHO CAME IN WITH THE GOLD

16) **B.**

Broccoli first went to Hollywood in 1932–33, around the time Hughes was shooting the movie classic *HELL'S ANGELS.* Bit by bit, Broccoli got his foot in the door, and in 1941, he was the assistant director on *THE OUT-LAW,* a Hughes project starring Jane Russell. Broccoli reportedly stayed friendly with Hughes until the billionaire died. As for Charles K. Feldman and Kevin McClory, they don't figure in the story until a little later.

17) **A.**

According to Broccoli, "There used to be a cartoon character named Abie Kabible, who was a little, fat, roly-poly kid. As a kid, I was a little roly-poly kind of chap. My cousin nicknamed me Abie Kabible, which was cut down to Kabible, and then they cut it down to Cubby."

18) **B.**

Although there were nine stories written by Fleming at the time of the deal, *CASINO ROYALE* had already been sold to another producer for $6,000, *MOONRAKER* had been sold to the Rank Organisation (*sic*) and *THUN-DERBALL*'s ownership was presumably still being determined in the courts.

19) **TRUE.**

Dana is Broccoli's wife and Jacqueline is Harry Saltzman's wife.

20) **C.**

The Long Island Casket Company was run by his cousin Augustine D'Orta. Several years before, Broccoli's first job was working on his Uncle Pasquale's broccoli farm and, as the legend goes, it really was Broccoli's family that was responsible for bringing that green vegetable to the United States.

21) **D.**

McClory was able to provide pictures taken a few years before in a special underwater cave that Fleming described in *THUNDERBALL.* While there

178

was certainly other evidence that awarded him the film rights to the story, this bit of photographic evidence was supposedly the clincher.

22) **A.**
CALL ME BWANA was made in 1963 and CHITTY CHITTY BANG BANG was made in 1968. CHITTY CHITTY BANG BANG was actually based on a story written by Ian Fleming, concerning the adventures of a magical car. The musical starred Dick Van Dyke and Sally Ann Howe.

23) **TRUE.**
After leaving the U.S. Navy, Broccoli first worked in Feldman's Hollywood office as an agent and Feldman later became the producer of CASINO ROYALE in 1967.

24) **C.**
It's precisely these "bumps" that make up a James Bond movie.

25) **A.**
Saltzman had seen Connery do a film called ON THE FIDDLE at around the same time Broccoli had seen him in DARBY O'GILL AND THE LITTLE PEOPLE. By the time they cast the first Bond, Roger Moore was doing THE SAINT for Lew Grade, and in spite of Fleming's previous requests for Jimmy Stewart, Richard Burton or James Mason, the producers felt it would be best to stick with a newcomer rather than going with a big name.

DOCTOR NO

26) **C.**
Le Cercle—Les Ambassadeurs, London is the name outside the casino where we first meet James Bond, Agent 007. Le Cercle was also the name of a now-defunct club founded by Ian Fleming in the mid-1930s, an eating place for old Etonians. The full name of the place was Le Cercle gastronomique et des jeux de hasard. One of its members was a certain John Fox-Strangways (the latter half of his family name was later appropriated by one of the characters in DOCTOR NO).

27) **A.**

28) **C.**

Bond has already met this woman at the casino earlier in the evening. It is during their initial conversation that the words "My name is Bond, James Bond" are first spoken.

29) **C.**

Dolores Keator played Mary, Zena Marshall played Miss Taro and Eileen Warwick was the film's hairstylist.

30) **FALSE.**

She appears in only one other Bond film, *FROM RUSSIA WITH LOVE.* The actress playing the part was a friend of director Terence Young, and when he wasn't involved with *GOLDFINGER,* neither was she. The idea behind her character was to provide 007 with a running romantic interest, someone he never had time to get down to serious business with because of his urgent assignments.

31) **A.**

32) **D.**

In the novel, "M" is concerned that Strangways and his secretary, Mary Trueblood, may have run off together. But in the movie, 007 is sent simply to find out what happened, and to see if their disappearance is connected to the disturbances involving American rockets.

33) **B.**

His previous mission, in *FROM RUSSIA WITH LOVE,* involved Rosa Klebb. During the dramatic climax, Bond is attacked by Klebb and her poison-tipped shoes. Unable to get his gun out of his pocket because of the stuck silencer, he is kicked in the shins and poisoned by Klebb. Although the Armorer does claim that Bond's Beretta is a "lady's" gun with no stopping power, "M" is more concerned with Bond's safety than with his faith in an old and trusted weapon.

34) **B.**

Born in Peking, he worked with the Tongs and Hip Sings in New York City. During the Tong wars, he stole a great deal of money, and was shot and left for dead. But, unbeknownst to his would-be assassins, his heart is on the wrong side of his body, so he lived.

35) **C.**

It was also his father's name.

36) **FALSE.**
Quarrel *is* killed by Doctor No's fire-breathing "Dragon," but on Crab Key, not Jamaica.

37) **B.**
The mysterious voice of Doctor No (played by Joseph Wiseman) tells Dent to kill Bond, and he provides a nasty little spider just for that purpose.

38) **B.**
The guano, or droppings, of the roseate spoonbills, is sold as fertilizer. At the time, this was a very profitable market, and it provides excellent cover for Doctor No's operation. It also comes in handy during Doctor No's burial when, at the end of the book, Bond dumps No into a mound of the stuff.

39) **B.**
Bond expressed hope that Honey not make a habit of doing this. In the movie, she says that her father was killed by Doctor No. Furthermore, although she doesn't stage shows like the one described in "A," she does claim to have witnessed such unusual events on the island of Jamaica.

40) **A.**
In the book, however, she *is* nude and singing "Marion."

41) **C.**
It seems the movie producers didn't feel this was a necessary ingredient for the screen version's success.

42) **D.**
She gives this address to 007 during their phone conversation, along with some fairly detailed directions.

43) **C.**
The good doctor seems to be checking his "patients." If you recall, Bond and Honey are given a sleeping drug in their coffee, and are in bed waiting to meet the good doctor.

44) **B.**
The scene was originally shot with crabs lying around Honey because that was what was called for in the novel, but ultimately it was deemed too gruesome for family viewing.

45) **B.**

The painting had recently been stolen from a major art gallery. This topical reference is one of the first in the series (see *MOONRAKER* for a film with topicality gone wild).

BE CAREFUL WITH THAT THING, WILL YA?

46) **A.**

The most current model of the Walther, pictured on the next page, has also made an appearance in a James Bond film. Robert Magee of Interarms, the company that manufactures the Walther, writes, "In at least one scene in *OCTOPUSSY* Roger Moore is shown using the P–5. I noticed this and it was pointed out to me as well by some of the real pros who are genuinely involved in international security. The P–5 is in caliber 9mm Parabellum and, while James Bond is on record as having used the PPK in caliber 7.65mm (.32 ACP), it's hard to believe that any agent worth his salt would be caught using anything less than a Walther in a 9mm Kurz (.380 ACP). The PPK pictured (question 46) is actually 9mm Kurz, but they all look the same anyway regardless of caliber."

47) **B.**

48) **C.**

In the movie, Scaramanga's weapon is made from a pen, cigarette case, cuff link and cigarette lighter. This entire mechanism was manufactured by Colibri Lighters of London.

49) **A.**

In *YOU ONLY LIVE TWICE,* at the office of the Japanese industrialist; in *ON HER MAJESTY'S SECRET SERVICE,* in the office of Gebrüder Gumbold; and in *MOONRAKER,* inside Hugo Drax's estate.

50) **D.**

Fleming had actually created the gimmick-filled attaché case for the novel *FROM RUSSIA WITH LOVE.* The major differences between the movie's case and the novel's is that there is no tear-gas device mentioned in the book; the silencer for Bond's Beretta (he hasn't been issued his Walther yet) is encased in a can of shaving cream, and a hidden compartment in the handle of the case contains cyanide death pills available at a moment's notice.

182

Walther Model P-5

(CREDIT: INTERARMS, Alexandria, VA.)

51) **B.**

His wristwatch not only gives off a "hyper-intensified electromagnetic field," it also serves as a tiny circular saw, which cuts Bond and Solitaire free before they are submerged into Kananga's private pool.

52) **B.**

In the opening scene, "Q" tells "M" about the lint, which is "to be secreted on an enemy agent and which will enable us to keep track of him." Aside from Bond's safe-cracking device and the portable xerox machine, this is the film's only gagdet.

53) **D.**

The rotating license plates were invented only for the film. The Colt .45 is kept in a trick compartment under the driver's seat. The lights of the car can be changed for day or night driving whenever he is following—or being followed by—someone.

54) **A–2, B–1, C–6, D–5, E–3, F–4.**

55) **B.**

The seagull appears in the pre-title sequence, when 007 is on a mission in Latin America to blow up the drug refinery. The alligator rears its head when Bond makes his way for the first time to Octopussy's palace.

FROM RUSSIA WITH LOVE

56) **B.**

57) **D.**

We witness the last three moves of the game. Kronsteen moves his Knight and takes Macadams's Bishop, Macadams moves his King to Rook 2, and then Kronsteen makes his final move. A moment passes, then Macadams (who's representing Canada and playing with the black pieces) knocks over his own King. For those who really want to know, the series was tied at 11½ games apiece.

58) **FALSE.**

Blofeld does not make an appearance in the novel *FROM RUSSIA WITH LOVE*, and when we do finally meet him in the books, he never seems to be holding a white cat. Presumably this is a film embellishment to give "Number One" some extra, added menace.

59) **A.**

In a magazine interview, Daniela Bianchi had this to say about her role: "I fall in love with him the moment my mission begins, so I don't have to slink, look over my shoulder and pass information. I'm a domesticated, home-loving spy, simply a woman in love." She also admitted that her voice was dubbed throughout the movie, her Italian accent being rather heavy.

60) **B.**

If you remember, Klebb says that Tatiana would only be shot if she tells anyone about the meeting or the mission. It seems a bit odd that Klebb doesn't make Tatiana swear never to tell anyone about the old colonel's sexual advances. In the novel, Klebb is far more forward, leaving the room to dress up in a nightgown and to look like, in Fleming's words, "the ugliest whore in the world." Tatiana runs away before anything further can happen between them.

61) **B.**

Says Bond, "I think it's just the right size. For me, that is."

62) **C.**

She calls no man "sir" except English kings and Winston Churchill. It is only her high regard for James Bond that prompts her to call him "s—."

63) **B.**

The nickname was given to him as a reference to his extreme "cool" while playing chess. General Grubozaboyschikov, known as "General G," was the head of SMERSH in Fleming's novel.

64) **B.**

65) **D.**

Leila was the name of the bellydancer, also featured at the gypsy camp, but not in this picture.

66) **B.**

67) **B.**

In fact, they were such fans of hers that they cast her in their own film *CALL ME BWANA,* which is advertised in the painting on the side of the wall. They obviously thought that a little free publicity couldn't hurt, and if you look closely in the upper left-hand corner of the screen, you can see the names of Harry Saltzman and Albert R. Broccoli.

68) **C.**

Unfortunately for both Kerim and the girl, a limpet mine goes off in his office before they can get down to some serious "salt mining."

69) **A.**

He indulged in these activities in a circus.

70) **B.**

After Grant slips Tatiana a sleeping pill and they return to their cabins, Grant pulls a gun and Bond says, "Red wine with fish, I should have known." Screenwriter Richard Maibaum once said of this line (and the line "She had her kicks"), "Those are my lines, the ones I claim and enjoy writing."

71) **C.**

She leaves them in a tiny compact, and Bond recovers them from the hands of a dead Bulgar lying at the foot of one of the pillars.

72) **D.**

Even though this is what Bond says to Tatiana on the tape, I found no other references to Bond or "M" carousing together anywhere, except perhaps at Blade's playing cards and cheating at bridge with Hugo Drax.

73) **C.**

Grant has a gun concealed inside his copy of Tolstoy's famous novel.

74) **C.**
When 007 passes out at the end of the novel, all we know is that Klebb has kicked him in the leg. We don't know what the poison is until the novel *DOCTOR NO,* when noted neurologist Sir James Molony tells "M" that Bond is very lucky to be alive. Fugu is a poison taken from the Japanese blowfish; the fish is sometimes served as a delicacy, but other times provides a deadly poison 200 thousand times more lethal than strychnine. In the novel *YOU ONLY LIVE TWICE,* Tiger Tanaka takes Bond to dinner, where 007 eats a finely prepared dish of fugu.

75) **FALSE.**
Bond tosses it into the Gulf of Venice, waving it good-bye.

HE WENT THATAWAY

76) **C.**
The DB VI is used in *ON HER MAJESTY'S SECRET SERVICE.*

77) **D.**

78) **B.**

79) **C.**
For those who need to keep score, the plate numbers were BMT–216A, 4711–EA62 and LU–6789.

80) **TRUE.**
According to the brochure supplied by Aston Martin, "The nearside lamp cluster hinges back and a hydraulic mechanism ejects oil onto the road." While this feature is used in *GOLDFINGER,* it was apparently modified to squirt water in *THUNDERBALL.* As the water is ejected, the scene dissolves into the opening credits sequence, which features water as its motif.

81) **A.**
The Aston Martin brochure refers to it as, "the offside lamp cluster," and says that it, "ejects nails specially designed so that no matter how they fall on the road, spikes always project upwards." Other defensive mechanisms on this car include: "Twin Browning Machine Guns fitted behind the car's front sidelights. The pressing of the console switch makes these lights hinge

forward and fire the guns. . . . (A) miniature revolving cutter extends 24 inches out from the nearside wheel hub, revolving in the opposite direction to the wheel spin. Designed to cut through the tyres of opposition cars. Front and rear bumpers extend hydraulically about 18″ for ramming purposes. Operated by a hydraulic ram, a bullet-proof steel plate (profiled to the exact contour of the luggage boot) can be raised to cover completely the rear window."

82) **D.**
Bond arrives with "Q" to assist Octopussy and her girls.

83) **B.**
After pretending to have drowned, Bond and Anya wait a few moments and then fire the missiles that destroy Naomi and her chopper in mid-air.

84) **C.**
Ken Adams and Derek Meddings were responsible for the design and special effects of this car. Lotus provided the six shells used by Perry Oceanographics to build the interior and exterior of each vehicle. The car was capable of cruising at 7.2 knots at a depth of 45 feet. Don Griffin of Perry Submarines is the driver substituting for Bond during the underwater sequences (though you can't really see him behind the Venetian blinds used in front of the car). In order to keep bubbles from filling the interior of the car, a "Perelli re-breather" was used to simulate the interior of a dry submersible. Griffin said that he often had to reshoot several scenes because the car moved too quickly for the cameras. In fact, the filming of the *Esprit* was scheduled to take ten days and wound up taking over ten weeks!

85) **D.**
The real car was a Citroen.

86) **D.**
As Bond and Melina try to elude their pursuers, they are forced down a narrow roadway and the car turns over. Since it's such a tiny thing, 007 and a few locals manage to turn it right side up in no time, and Bond and Melina continue their escape.

87) **C.**
Bond arrived in America without his own car, so during the chase through Las Vegas he drives Tiffany's red Mustang.

88) **A–5, B–2, C–3, D–4, E–1**

89) **C.**
In *FROM RUSSIA WITH LOVE* when he fights Grant; in *LIVE AND LET DIE* when he fights Tee-Hee; in *THE SPY WHO LOVED ME* when he fights Jaws; and in *OCTOPUSSY* when he fights a variety of Kamal Khan's thugs and circus extras.

90) **B.**
Bond uses it during the last part of the film, when he leaves the American sub and heads for Stromberg's hideout in search of Anya. The Wetbike is powered by a two-cycle, 50-horsepower engine, which gets the 350-pound machine up and running to speeds of around 30 m.p.h. It's seven and one half feet long, two feet wide and has a hull three and one half feet across. And should a driver fall off, the machine automatically shuts off and rights itself.

GOLDFINGER

91) **C.**
He quickly turns around and is finally able to subdue the intruder by tossing an electric heater into a full bathtub, frying the man to death. Per Bond: "Shocking, quite shocking."

92) **C.**
A man named Ramirez had been smuggling heroin in bananas prior to Bond's demolition of his refinery. The notion that Bond was in Latin America dealing with drug smugglers before meeting Goldfinger is actually taken from the novel. While Fleming never actually wrote a sequence with Bond in Mexico, he does have Bond recall the incident in Mexico that preceded his arrival in Miami. The filmmakers took this tale and turned it into an exciting pre-title sequence for the movie.

93) **B.**
Miss Nolan isn't listed in the credits, but this handy bit of information can be found in the *Playboy* magazine articles about James Bond.

94) **C.**
While Simmons is the name used in the film, Du Pont is the name in the book. Bond had actually met a Mr. Du Pont in the *CASINO ROYALE* story, playing *baccarat* in the same game as 007 and Le Chiffre. A man

named Bob Simmons, coincidentally, is responsible for most of the stunt work in a majority of the James Bond films.

95) **FALSE.**

Bond hates tea and thinks it one of the reasons for the fall of the British Empire. However, he toys with the idea of writing a book called *Stay Alive!* It is supposed to contain all the best secrets of unarmed combat available to the Secret Service. Unfortunately, he never gets around to starting it.

96) **B.**

Drinking warm champagne, according to Jimmy Bond, is like listening to the Beatles without earmuffs. Remember, this was in 1964, and the Beatles were just beginning to revolutionize pop music, so please forgive 007.

97) **A.**

About her bizarre makeup, Miss Eaton said, "It makes you hot all over, darling, and it takes about an hour to get it off."

98) **B.**

Jill's sleeping with 007 is a major "no-no" as far as Goldfinger was concerned. According to the *novel,* however, Goldfinger does paint girls gold for sexual stimulation.

99) **B.**

The only other reference to Agent 008 appears in the novel *MOON-RAKER,* where we learn that his name is Bill and he has been on assignment in Peenemunde, the site of the Nazi V–2 experiments.

100) **C.**

Sax Rohmer, choice "B," was the author of the Fu Manchu stories, of which Ian Fleming had been a devoted fan as a youth.

101) **D.**

102 **B.**

Goldfinger's other henchmen are also Korean.

103) **C.**

Goldfinger uses a Slazenger #1, but during the game (at hole 17) Bond stands on it, replacing it with a Slazenger #7. Goldfinger doesn't notice the switch as he hits the ball off the tee for the last hole. In the novel, Goldfinger uses a Dunlop 65, #1, which Bond switches to a #7. James Bond uses a Penfold Hearts golf ball in both the novel and the movie.

104) **B.**
But Goldfinger tells Bond not to worry about what the owner will think; he, Goldfinger, owns the club.

105) **C.**
Bond overhears Goldfinger use this phrase in a conversation with the Oriental back at the Swiss smelting plant, and later uses it to save himself from death.

106) **B.**

107) **A.**

108) **C.**
Oddjob isn't killed inside Fort Knox, but is killed aboard the plane with Goldfinger, Pussy and Bond. James Bond has always been somewhat leery of flying, but nonetheless shoots the hole in the window through which Oddjob is sucked out. Later, Bond and Goldfinger tangle in a fight, each man trying to choke the other. Of course 007 wins and strangles his opponent.

109) **C.**

110) **D.**
During the mad chase through Auric Enterprises in Switzerland, Bond zigzags up and down the alleyways around the factories (which are actually the sound stages at Pinewood Studios in England). As he approaches a blinding light he shoots the gun, accomplishing nothing since he's only shooting at a large mirror.

SURE IT LOOKS EASY

111) **B.**
Stuntman Jerry Comeaux performs this stunt, which had to be carefully prepared and timed. Operating a 585-pound Glastron GT-150 boat, Comeaux drives the specially rigged boat up a ramp situated at a curve in

the middle of a 50-foot-wide canal. Hurtling at a speed of around 56 m.p.h., Comeaux takes the boat up the ramp and sails for a distance of 110 feet, clearing first water and then land at a height of 12 feet. A crowd of about 300 cheered his landing on the other side of the canal in the Louisiana Bayou.

112) **B.**

In *GOLDFINGER,* Goldfinger falls from his own plane, and in *YOU ONLY LIVE TWICE,* Tanaka sends a helicopter to pick up a black sedan following Aki and 007, dropping the car (passengers and all) into the Sea of Japan. In *MOONRAKER,* the pilot of the plane falls without a parachute during the pre-title sequence, and in *FOR YOUR EYES ONLY,* the "bald man in the wheelchair with the white cat" is dropped from a helicopter into a smokestack. In *OCTOPUSSY,* Gobinda falls from Kamal Khan's plane during a fight with 007.

113) **A.**

With its steering column repositioned in the center, the car makes the jump in just a few seconds. The exact angle of the ramp and the weight of the car had been previously worked out on a computer at Cornell University.

114) **FALSE.**

The location of the stunt is actually 20 miles north of the Arctic Circle, on Baffin Island, Canada. Stunt arranger Rick Sylvester performed the 3,000-foot jump before the cameras of second-unit director John Glen. The jump is based on a magazine advertisement for Canadian Club.

115) **B.**

This occurs during Bond's first escape from Blofeld's mountain-top retreat. In *FOR YOUR EYES ONLY,* Bond is forced to ski without any ski *poles.*

116) **B.**

Director Richard Talmadge, 67 at the time, stage-managed the chaos. A veteran of the silent screen *(DANGER AHEAD)* and the stunt arranger for *HOW THE WEST WAS WON,* he was responsible for coordinating the climactic madness that took two months to shoot. At one point, after witnessing a scene in which clothing is on fire and roulette wheels fly through the air, Lloyd's of London panicked and suspended their insurance policy.

117) **C.**

The scene inside the Kuramae Kokugian sumo hall in Tokyo took three days to shoot and featured 2,000 hired extras to fill the ringside seats. In the rest of the 10,000-seat arena sat those James Bond fans who had responded to an advertisement for "extras."

118) **FALSE.**

Maurice Patchett was a London bus driver who instructed Roger Moore on the finer points of driving a 55-ton London Transport double-decker bus. When the bus rams into the bridge (which was specially constructed by the film crew for the sequence), Jane Seymour is strapped below as the top is sliced off.

119) **A–1, B–8, C–7, D–9, E–3, F–5, G–6, H–4, I–2, J–10**

120) **C.**

Bond fights Peter Franks in the elevator on the way up to Tiffany Case's flat. Guess who wins.

THUNDERBALL

121) **TRUE.**

While the credits list the name as Boiter, Boivard is the name actually used in the scene. Colonel Jacques Boivard is presumably the man in the coffin at the beginning of the film, so when 007 punches him in the face, he's punching someone who is supposed to be dead. The location of this fight scene is the Chateau d'Anet, near Paris, France. It was built by King Henry II for Diane de Poitiers.

122) **C.**

Mr. Doleman was also used by producer Harry Saltzman in Len Deighton's Harry Palmer films, where he plays Michael Caine's boss, a man named Ross.

123) **C.**

Although the room is certainly steamy, we see the name "irrigation room" stenciled on the door after Bond is through with her.

124) **C.**

125) **D.**

126) **C.**

The black circle with the spike cutting through it was the symbol used by the Osato Chemical Corporation in *YOU ONLY LIVE TWICE.*

127) **B.**

128) **B.**

129) **A.**

As Largo enters the front of the building, we can see the Eiffel Tower in the background. The street location is the one given in the novel.

130) **A.**

In the novel, F.I.R.C.O. is the name that serves as the cover for SPEC-TRE. In French, it stands for *Fraternité Internationale de la Résistance Contre l'Opression,* which roughly translates to answer C.

131) **C.**

The *Sonderdienst* was part of Nazi Germany's Gestapo, an elite corps within this elite corps.

132) **C.**

Born in the Polish city of Gdynia, located north of Gdansk along the Sea of Danzig, Blofeld's father was Polish and his mother Greek.

133) **D.**

Although she was born in Italy, Domino studied acting at the Royal Academy of Dramatic Arts in London. During their meeting inside the casino in Nassau, she tells Bond how much she would like to quit smoking, but then goes on (for almost four pages in the book) about the history of the sailor on the packet of Players cigarettes.

134) **B.**

The arrival of the atomic scientist prevents Largo from perpetrating his method of torture.

135) **B.**

In the novel, Bond and Largo are fighting underwater when Domino shoots her former lover with a harpoon gun. In the film, Largo must wait until he's aboard the *Disco Volante* before Domino can spear him.

136) **C.**

Bond knows someone else is there because of a tape recorder he's hidden in his room to pick up the sounds of uninvited guests. On the tape, he hears someone enter and walk around, but he never hears the sounds of the man leaving. Bond finds him, and when the thug won't talk, Bond sends him back to Largo, who feeds him to the pet shark he keeps in his swimming pool.

137) **B.**

Vargas is harpooned by 007, and Quist is the unfortunate soul who's fed to the sharks in the episode discussed in question 136.

138) **FALSE.**

When the *Disco Volante* separates from its "cocoon," we can see that it was actually registered in Panama.

139) **A.**

140) **C.**

After Bond and Domino jump off the doomed *Disco Volante,* Felix Leiter drops a life raft from a circling airplane. Once they are safely aboard the raft, Bond inflates a large weather balloon and the plane picks up the balloon, with Bond and Domino hanging on tight.

FIRST WE BLOW UP THE EARTH

141) **A–1, B–5, C–6, D–10, E–8, F–4, G–11, H–3, I–7, J–2, K–9**

142) **B.**

143) **D.**

Lotte Lenya was married to Kurt Weill, the famous German composer of such musicals as *Three Penny Opera* and *Lady in the Dark.*

144) **D.**

Although we've seen the hands of someone called "Number One," and have even heard him speak, we don't see the face of Blofeld until Sean Connery arrives inside the volcano headquarters of SPECTRE, where Donald Pleasance turns to Bond and introduces himself as Ernst Stavro Blofeld.

145) **FALSE.**
When Ian Fleming and Kevin McClory first began working on an original screenplay for James Bond, Fatima Blush was created as a deadly double-agent working for SPECTRE. It's taken her over 20 years to finally make it to the silver screen.

146) **B.**

147) **C.**
Anthony Dawson plays Professor Dent in *DOCTOR NO,* and his hands are seen stroking the white cat in *FROM RUSSIA WITH LOVE.* The voice of actor Eric Pohlman is heard when "Number One" speaks.

148) **B.**
If you look very closely when Stromberg presses the button that destroys the helicopter of the two scientists who helped develop the submarine tracking system, you can see the webbing between the thumb and forefinger on his right hand. In the movie novelisation, written by Christopher Wood, much more is made of Stromberg's aquatic peculiarities—with an emphasis on how his face would squish up into a red blob with just a tiny hole for a mouth whenever he lost his temper. This was obviously too much to ask for on screen.

149) **D.**
Le Chiffre has just finished torturing Evelyn Tremble when an angry agent of SMERSH appears inside one of his television monitors. Because Le Chiffre has lost too much money at the gambling table, SMERSH has ordered his death; the gunman sticks his arm through the screen and shoots Orson Welles (who played the rather heavy heavy) between the eyes.

150) **C.**
Four full-faced actors, plus one who supplies the hands of Blofeld, another who supplies the voice, and the man who appears in the pre-title sequence in *FOR YOUR EYES ONLY.*

CASINO ROYALE

151) **C.**
This is the title on the first copies of the novel published in the United States by Macmillan in March, 1954.

152) **FALSE.**

Everything in this description is correct except that there are *three* gold bands on his cigarettes, not two.

153) **D.**

The incident involving the Japanese cipher clerk is based on a World War II story about Fleming himself. Attached to the New York branch of the British Secret Service, he gathered intelligence with Sir William Stephenson. On one particular assignment, Stephenson broke into the Japanese Consulate in Rockfeller Center, "borrowed" some important code books belonging to the Japanese, copied them and returned them before they were even missed. Fleming exaggerates this event, turning it into a major sniper attack described by 007 in *CASINO ROYALE.*

154) **B.**

Miss Kerr got into *CASINO ROYALE* quite by accident. She stopped by the set one day to say hello to director John Huston, was roped into playing the part of "M" 's wife, and ended up staying for a few months' worth of work. According to the script, she and "M" (played by director Huston) had 12 daughters.

155) **B.**

Of course Bond does eat a haggis with the whole household, he does play medicine ball and he does shoot grouse. However, these are mere distractions provided by the opposition to thwart his more vital errands.

156) **C.**

Bond's lions greet the arrival of Charles Boyer, William Holden, Kurt Kazner and John Huston—emissaries of France, America, Russia and Britain—when they arrive to try to talk Bond out of retirement.

157) **B.**

158) **C.**

159) **B.**

160) **A.**

In one of her earliest screen appearances, Miss Bisset seduces Sellers by dropping a mickey in his champagne. Unfortunately for his character, nothing else happens between them.

161) **C.**

At the Mata Hari School for Spies, a sale of pornographic pictures is under way when Mata Bond arrives by taxi from London. The school is situated along the Berlin Wall; after Mata and her taxi driver leave, an explosion rips through the wall and hundreds of East German refugees pile into the West. Vladek Sheybal (who plays Kronsteen in *FROM RUSSIA WITH LOVE*), makes an appearance, helplessly shooting at the disappearing taxi.

162) **C.**

Peter Sellers is in the middle of his mind-trip, when 104 Scottish Highlanders, in kilts and playing bagpipes, appear in the fog. As he rushes about, he stops a man and asks, "Aren't you Peter O'Toole?" To which Peter O'Toole replies, "No, I'm Richard Burton." O'Toole himself was roped into appearing in *CASINO ROYALE* quite by accident. When he dropped by the set to wish Ursula Andress a happy birthday, he put on a kilt and picked up a bagpipe for what he thought was a *rehearsal* of the Highlanders scene. Unbeknownst to him, the cameras were rolling. The producer paid him a full case of champagne for his services.

163) **A.**

Miss Andress thought that movie stars like to "ride on top of elephants," and so requested that this costume be made. When Peter Sellers nixed the idea of an elephant scene, the costume already existed, so they let her use it in the spy code room sequence.

164) **TRUE.**

While Wolf Mankowitz, John Law and Michael Sayers received final credit for the screenplay, others who contributed pieces to the concoction included Ben Hecht, Joseph Heller, Terry Southern, Billy Wilder, Peter Sellers and, most probably, Woody Allen. During production there was never any full-length script available to anyone other than Charles Feldman, which led Woody Allen to surmise that there was a mysterious house writer locked up in some basement putting the bits and pieces of *CASINO ROYALE* together.

165) **A.**

166) **C.**

"This pill contains 400 tiny little time pills. They go off in the body in little explosions, causing a chain reaction and turn the person into a walking atomic bomb." Woody Allen, as Jimmy Bond, Sir James Bond's nephew, swallows it when the Detainer, played by Daliah Lavi, slips it into his drink. As for Doctor Noah's baccillus, that's an altogether different concoction.

167) **B.**

168) **C.**

169) **A.**
One had to stick one's finger into the tiger's ear to make the elevator travel down to SMERSH headquarters beneath the casino.

170) **D.**

THOSE LIPS, THOSE EYES . . .

171) **C.**

172) **C.**
Solitaire was a virgin whose mystical powers to read the future could not survive a single act of lovemaking.

173) **B.**
Believe it or not, that's all.

174) **D.**
As soon as she graduated from high school, actress Mie (pronounced Me-eh and meaning "beautiful twig") Hama became a bus conductor. For a year she collected fares on a bus line in Kawasaki, Tokyo, until she was discovered by a pair of Japanese filmmakers. She was fired by the bus company because she failed to tell her boss she'd be busy making a movie for a few weeks.

175) **D.**
In *GOLDFINGER* it's Jill Masterson, in *THUNDERBALL* it's Fiona, in *YOU ONLY LIVE TWICE* it's Aki, in *ON HER MAJESTY'S SECRET SERVICE* it's Tracy, in *LIVE AND LET DIE* it's Rosie, in *THE MAN WITH THE GOLDEN GUN* it's Andrea, in *MOONRAKER* it's Corrine and in *FOR YOUR EYES ONLY* it's Lisl. For those who want to include

Plenty O'Toole in this list, remember that, while she does eventually "buy the farm" she never actually shares 007's bed.

176) **A.**

177) **B.**

178) **A.**

179) **D.**

180) **B and D.**
Honor Blackman left "The Avengers" to play Pussy Galore in *GOLD-FINGER*. She was Cathy Gale, John Steed's partner in the early episodes of the series, and was replaced by Diana Rigg as Mrs. Emma Peel. Rigg played Tracy in *ON HER MAJESTY'S SECRET SERVICE*.

YOU ONLY LIVE TWICE

181) **A.**

182) **C.**
This is a glaring error on the part of screenwriter Roald Dahl, but the producers let it slip through, so guilt must be shared.

183) **A.**

184) **TRUE.**
When the Russian spaceship is launched, the sky is bright blue and a palm tree can be seen waving in the foreground. (This is obviously stock film footage taken in Florida).

185) **A.**

186) **C.**
"I'm glad you got it right," says Henderson.

187) **TRUE.**
What is doubly surprising is that 007 doesn't correct Henderson and order his vodka martini as usual: "shaken, not stirred." In an early novel, Bond describes his perfect martini as containing three measures of gin,

one of vodka, half a measure of "Kina Lillet," shaken very well until ice cold and served in a deep champagne goblet with a slice of lemon peel.

188) **B.**

189) **C.**
It is designed to let the inhabitant know when someone is approaching. There is no possible way to walk on it without making some kind of noise.

190) **B.**
Miss Moneypenny is delighted to teach Bond this code and asks him to test it out on her. But he assures "M" 's ever-faithful secretary that he won't forget it.

191) **A.**
One of Osato's men tries to poison 007 using a thin thread and poison that will drip down from the ceiling into Bond's mouth. At the last moment, Bond turns over, and Aki moves directly underneath the path of the thread and poison.

192) **D.**
It contains all sorts of plants and fish that provide a perfect setting for suicides.

193) **B.**
A dermitone is described as a sharp knife used by plastic surgeons.

194) **C.**

195) **C.**

196) **B.**
Jupiter 16 is the name of the flight and, as can be seen on the screen, the spacecraft is one of the Gemini series.

197) **B.**
Their marriage isn't official because Bond gave the priest an incorrect name, as Kissy reminds a rather pushy 007 when he wants to consummate their marriage on the first night of their "honeymoon."

198) **B.**

199) **C.**

200) **B.**

Bond and Kissy are embracing in a tiny life raft when a submarine comes up directly underneath it. "M" is on board, and he tells Miss Moneypenny to tell 007 to come below and report. She says, "It'll be a pleasure, sir."

IT WAS SO BIG THAT . . .

201) **C.**

Soundstage "007" was dedicated in a ceremony held on December 5, 1976. It measures 336 feet long with an exterior tank of 38 feet, giving it an overall length of 374 feet, a width of 160 feet and a height of 53 feet. Until that time, the largest set ever built was the volcano set used in *YOU ONLY LIVE TWICE*—120 feet high to accommodate the 66-foot-tall *Intruder* spacecraft (which actually was able to elevate off its launch platform), with 8,000 railway ties, 200 miles of steel tubing and 250,000 square yards of canvas. The space station built for *MOONRAKER* cost $500,000 to build, and was the largest single set ever built in a French film studio. As for *CASINO ROYALE*'s Taj Mahal, it cost $30,000 and was never actually used during the shooting of the picture.

202) **A.**

German-born Ken Adam has been production designer for *DOCTOR NO, GOLDFINGER, THUNDERBALL, YOU ONLY LIVE TWICE, DIAMONDS ARE FOREVER, THE SPY WHO LOVED ME* and *MOONRAKER*. He's also designed the films *CHITTY CHITTY BANG BANG, SLEUTH* and *DOCTOR STRANGELOVE,* and he won an Academy Award for his work on *BARRY LYNDON*.

203) **TRUE.**

Some aerial footage and nearby exterior location shooting was done near the real site in Kentucky, but Ken Adam designed his own interior and exterior on the lot at Pinewood Studios, England, at a cost of approximately $500,000.

204) **B.**

205) **FALSE.**
While searching through the Alps for a possible location, the producers happened upon the revolving restaurant atop Schilthorn Peak in Murren, Switzerland. It wasn't the actual site described by Fleming in his book, but it looked similar. Situated 10,000 feet up the mountain peak, the restaurant revolves 360 degrees every hour. After the producers decided on this location, a helicopter platform had to be built to fit the terrain. At a cost of over $100,000, Eon Productions built the landing pad at the restaurant in exchange for shooting privileges. After the crew completed location filming, the restaurant was renamed Piz Gloria (meaning Glorious Peak) in honor of the Fleming title it assumed in *ON HER MAJESTY'S SECRET SERVICE.* To this day, it still bears that name.

206) **B.**
Vesper Lynd's London flat features these works of art, along with a portable bathroom (with bidet) capable of being taken anywhere.

207) **C.**
Also polished off were 27,000 eggs, 40,500 bread rolls and 400 journalists! Over 35,000 still pictures were taken by the unit photographer.

208) **C.**
After 17 weeks of location shooting, the Bond cast and crew took over the Italian ski resort of Cortina to complete some of the most exciting snow and ski action sequences ever shot. Unfortunately, nobody told the weatherman, and Cortina experienced its lightest recorded snowfall since 1956. Producer Broccoli examined his budget. Fearing a cost overrun if no shooting was accomplished at all, and eager to keep the approximately 250 members of the Bond team busy and earning their paychecks, he hired six trucks to make about 45 trips to nearby mountain peaks in order to carry back enough snow to fill a few scenes (including the sequences shot in the main shopping center of Cortina d'Ampezzo).

209) **D.**

210) **FALSE.**
The Maharajah of Udaipur is a rich man, but he didn't have Octopussy's ceremonial barge floating at his dock, so the art department had to make one up. Production designer Peter Lamont did not have enough time to build the barge in London and ship it to the location, so he and his team

decided to use two derelict ceremonial barges that were floating in the marshes of Lake Pichola, India. They took parts from both ships and, with the help of art department magic, turned a rotting hulk into a wonderfully colorful sailing vessel. It is true, however, that the Maharajah gave permission to the 007 team to do location shooting at various sites throughout Udaipur.

ON HER MAJESTY'S SECRET SERVICE

211) **B.**

Although Bond is driving along in his car wearing a hat and smoking a cigarette when he first appears on screen, we don't know for sure who's playing 007. (Well, actually we do, but we don't yet know what he *looks* like.) It is only when he follows Tracy out onto the sandy beach and identifies himself that we see George Lazenby.

212) **D.**

213) **TRUE.**

George Lazenby was an Australian model without any previous acting experience. A friend who was a talent agent told Lazenby that some producers were looking for a new James Bond, and suggested he try out for the part. After a ten-minute acting lesson given to him by a "Radio Caroline" announcer, Lazenby set to work. He found Sean Connery's tailor and bought a suit that Connery had ordered but never picked up. He next went to Sean's barber and got himself a "James Bond" haircut. (Coincidentally, Cubby Broccoli was seated near him, getting a haircut himself. According to Lazenby, the two did not know each other at the time, but the story later circulated that Broccoli had discovered him at the barber.) After Lazenby felt confident that he looked just right, he went to the office of the casting director, who was on the phone with Harry Saltzman at the time. The casting director told Saltzman that someone who looked right had just walked in, and Lazenby was soon on his way to meet with Saltzman himself. Four months and numerous tests later, a final tryout was made with a stunt man, wherein Lazenby had to "do a fight." During the test, having never worked with a stuntman before, Lazenby punched him in the nose, thereby convincing the producers to hire him.

214) **FALSE.**
George Baker provided the voice of the man who played Sir Hilary Bray, and dubbed all of Lazenby's scenes in which Bond pretends to be Sir Hilary.

215) **D.**

216) **A.**

217) **A.**
As Bond is taken through the outer office of Draco's headquarters, he hears a midget janitor whistling while he sweeps.

218) **C.**
This is the literal meaning, although the implied meaning is that something should be kept secret. The idea is to keep the news "in your mouth, behind your teeth."

219) **B.**
Since *THUNDERBALL*, the cinematic 007 had been looking everywhere for Blofeld, and it is "M" who feels that the search is futile. In the novel, Bond resigns because he is tired of wasting his time searching for Blofeld, but "M" wants him to remain confined solely to Operation Bedlam (the name given to the hunt for Blofeld).

220) **A.**

221) **A.**

222) **A.**
Located in West Germany, Augsburg is "fair ground," where Blofeld could be arrested by any number of organizations friendly to 007. As it stands, Blofeld is protected in Switzerland.

223) **C.**
She pulls Tracy aside during Draco's birthday celebration and gives her this bit of news. Tracy is enraged and storms off, but a genuinely sympathetic James Bond follows her out to her car, where she's found crying. They embrace, and what follows is a lyrical love montage—a collection of sights all over Europe as Bond and Tracy fall in love.

224) **B.**

225) **C.**

As she writes her room number on his thigh with lipstick, 007 covers for her with the remark, "I feel a slight stiffness coming on."

226) **B.**

He's actually describing the family herald belonging to Bray, the man he is portraying at the time.

227) **A.**

228) **D.**

According to the novel, the ceremony took place at 10:30 A.M. at the British Consulate in Munich.

229) **A.**

Bond tells Draco in the early part of the film that he doesn't want his money, and he keeps his word. In the novel, 007 allows the saddened Draco a moment of parental joy when he tells the old man that if he and Tracy have children or are ever really strapped for cash, they'll call on him.

230) **B.**

ANOTHER OPENING, ANOTHER SHOW

231) **B.**

On May 6, 1967, every available policeman in the Boston area was called into the honky-tonk section of the city to contain a riot that broke out among the hundreds of moviegoers. Six people were taken to the hospital and 12 arrests were made. It all happened when a movie house offered free admission to a preview of *CASINO ROYALE* for anyone who showed up wearing a trench coat.

232) **A.**

Sleepy-eyed high school students and bar patrons with no place else to go made up the majority of the audience. A few parents who were roped into driving their kids to the theater ended up staying for the screening and, according to the theater manager, "The audience was orderly and awake, for the most part."

233) **B.**

According to an article in the New York *Times, GOLDFINGER* was banned in Israel after six weeks because of actor Gert Frobe's admission, in a newspaper interview, that he had been a member of the Nazi party. At the time, the then-52-year-old actor said that although he joined the party in 1929 at the age of 19, he had helped a Jewish woman survive persecution by hiding her in his apartment for the duration of the war. Censorship of the film was possible because of a 1956 Israeli Cabinet decision that outlawed German-made films and those that used actors who had been wartime Nazis.

234) **FALSE.**

None of the Bond films has ever played the Soviet Union. However, despite this obvious ban on Bond, Soviet film critic Anna Martynova wrote a scathing review in the Soviet weekly *Literaturnaya Gazeta* after screening a copy of *MOONRAKER:* "Although the Bond plots had changed in complexion since such openly anti-Soviet movies as 'From Russia With Love' in the early 1960's, they still answer the dictates of bourgeois ideologists. . . . 'Moonraker' continues the tradition of all 11 Bondmania films, it has not only the cosmic but also the earthy values of mass culture—namely sex, violence and super-individualism." Adding that the Bond films have made approximately $500 million in "pure profit" (her words), she concludes, "It is the unlimited stupidity of James Bond films that explains their vitality." *That*'s telling us.

235) **B.**

At the *Galeries Lafayettes* in Paris, a special boutique was set up specifically to sell James Bond–related merchandise. Black briefcases were piled high around Sean Connery's Aston Martin, and English James Bond shirts were sold that had special messages written on fancy letterhead embossed with the emblem "On Her Majesty's Secret Service." A chief buyer said, "Happily, this promotion coincides with the English style and image of a virile man of action." While women were being told what to buy in order to "become fit for James Bond," a press release stated, "The Bond cult is purely psychological."

236) **B.**

237) **C.**

DOCTOR NO cost a little less than a million dollars to make, whereas *MOONRAKER* cost over thirty million dollars. (*OCTOPUSSY* also cost approximately thirty million dollars.)

238) **A.**

According to a statement made by Executive Producer Michael G. Wilson in *Variety, GOLDFINGER* has been seen by an estimated 84 percent of the available world audience.

239) **A and B.**

At the Pittsburgh *Press,* editors actually put shorts on the lady in the picture. The legs in the photograph belong to Joyce Bartle, a New York model who has filled stocking ads for Hanes, L'Eggs and Givenchy.

240) **A.**

Maurice Binder designed the titles for all the Bond films except two (*FROM RUSSIA WITH LOVE* and *GOLDFINGER* were designed by Robert Brownjohn). During a press conference at the Museum of Modern Art in New York City, Binder said that for the first gunsight logo, designed for *DOCTOR NO,* stuntman Bob Simmons appears in the sights rather than Sean Connery. But all subsequent logos feature either Connery (with or without a hat), George Lazenby (with a hat), or Roger Moore (without a hat). A .38 calibre long-barreled revolver is used. The opening had to be changed every time the scope of the film size was changed.

DIAMONDS ARE FOREVER

241) **A.**

This is also the method used in the movie.

242) **C.**

243) **C.**

007 identifies the sherry as an 1851 Solero, correctly advising "M" that he is not referring to the vintage of the sherry, but to the vintage of the wine on which the sherry was based.

244) **B.**

Fortunately for Bond, "Q" has given him false fingerprints, which fool Miss Case.

245) **C.**

Felix Leiter informs 007 of Tiffany's unfortunate past. Her mother ran a whorehouse in San Francisco; when she decided to stop paying protection money to the local mob, a gang of hoodlums arrived at the house and, ignoring the "professionals," gang-raped Tiffany. The 16-year-old stole her mother's money and ran away from home, eventually becoming an alcoholic but never again going near a man.

246) **B.**
She's not too thrilled to be playing childish games, but the balloon-booth manager fills her balloon with water so that she can win a stuffed animal (which just happens to be filled with jewels).

247) **D.**
He's using an electromagnetic r.p.m. controller, and winning a fortune up and down an entire row of slot machines.

248) **C.**
Bond calls "Q" from Tiffany's Amsterdam flat to thank him for the fingerprints while, in the background at "Q" Branch, a large contraption containing six enormous rockets is being loaded into the famous automobile.

249) **B.**
In the book his golf ball brand is a Dunlop 65, the same brand used by Goldfinger.

250) **A.**
In the novel, Bond is taken off for a beating by a few of Mr. Spang's henchmen who are under orders to make it an "80 percenter."

251) **D.**
The Slumber Funeral Home was created for the movie.

252) **B.**

253) **C.**
Shady Tree is the Vegas comedian who gets killed in his dressing room by Mr. Wint and Mr. Kidd.

254) **B.**

255) **C.**
Spang owns a ghost town, located in the Spectre mountain range, complete with old-time saloon, main street and hotel. It even features a

run-down vintage train system, which was used for traveling out into the desert.

256) **C.**
The thug who tossed her out the window in Bond's hotel room added, "I didn't know there was a pool down there." Plenty O'Toole was played by Lana Wood, the sister of actress Natalie Wood, who is currently appearing on a CBS Television network soap opera.

257) **D.**

258) **FALSE.**
While the girls do almost drown 007 in the pool at Whyte's summer house, James Bond has the situation well under control by the time Felix arrives with the Feds. In fact, he almost drowns the two girls single-handedly.

259) **A.**

260) **B.**
In Maibaum's version of the script, the villain isn't Blofeld but supposedly is Auric Goldfinger's twin brother. When a bunch of Las Vegas gambling big shots are double-crossed by Goldfinger II, they chase him in a variety of boats across Lake Mead, until 007 catches up with him atop Hoover Dam. Tom Mankiewicz, the other writer on *DIAMONDS ARE FOREVER,* had yet another ending in mind for the picture. With Blofeld as the villain, Bond would chase him to Mexico, where he'd be granulated in a salt mine.

THERE'S A PLACE FOR US, SOMEWHERE

261) **D.**

262) **D.**
Also known as Khow-Ping-Kan, this Thai location is a national shrine, and was used for actual location shooting for *THE MAN WITH THE GOLDEN GUN.* With the assistance of the Tourist Organization of Thailand, Eon Productions scouted the site and was given permission to clean the place up to make it usable as a movie set. However, the government of Thailand changed hands while the shooting was going on, and

the new regime didn't recognize the permission granted by the previous regime. They accused the Bond crew of desecrating the sacred island. Things were eventually smoothed out, and shooting was completed. But according to Cubby Broccoli, there was no real need for the ruckus: "All we did was clean it up. The place was littered with Coca Cola bottles."

263) **FALSE.**

The location used for this sequence was the R.A.F. base at Upper Heyford, England. The home of the 20th Tactical Fighter Wing of the U.S. Air Force, it served as the double for the U.S. Air Force base in Feldstadt, West Germany. Just outside of London is the R.A.F. Northolt airbase, which served as the Latin American air base and horse-riding ring used in the pre-title sequence.

264) **A.**

Owned by aristocratic socialite Minnie Simpson, the estate was located 18 miles to the east of Fleming's own "Goldeneye" in Oracabessa. Mrs. Simpson had once turned down an offer of $1,000,000 from Henry Ford, who wanted to buy the place, but because she was such a James Bond enthusiast, she gladly lent her estate as a location for the filmmakers.

265) **C.**

266) **A.**

Director Terence Young was trying to get a shot of Sean Connery running into the Sirkeci railroad station near the Galata Bridge in Istanbul, but there were too many civilian bystanders. With the help of the local police, one of his stuntmen went across the street and started shouting from a third-story window, which gradually drew the crowd away. A fire engine was also part of the ploy, and when that came screaming around the corner, the crowd moved over to see what was going on. Moving quickly, Young, Connery and the rest of the crew got the shot they wanted in one, fast take.

267) **C.**

The monks decided that, since the film depicted scenes of sex, terror and violence, they didn't want their famous monastery to be seen in the film. Despite offers of payment from the production team, the monks draped the monastery with all the sheets and toilet paper they could find. Fortunately for director John Glen and producer Cubby Broccoli, the side of

Meteora they needed had already been filmed, so all they had to do was shoot around the camouflage.

268) **D.**

269) **B.**

In the tiny fishing village of Akime, Japan, located 720 miles from Tokyo, Eon Productions paid 400 local fisherman approximately $100,000 to keep their boats on the beach during location shooting. The fishermen usually earned about $150 each from their daily catch, so the deal suited them fine.

270) **D.**

LIVE AND LET DIE

271) **A.**

Madeline Smith plays Miss Caruso, a missing Italian agent who is in bed with James Bond when "M" and Miss Moneypenny arrive at his flat.

272) **C.**

At the end of *CASINO ROYALE,* the novel that preceded *LIVE AND LET DIE,* an agent of SMERSH arrived to kill Le Chiffre. Although the Russian didn't have orders to kill James Bond, he did leave a mark on the back of Bond's right hand—an inverted "M" carved into 007's flesh with a stiletto. The mark was actually a crude drawing of the Russian letter for "SCH," the first letter in the Russian word for spy: *spion.* It would identify 007 as a spy to all those in the profession. *Smyert Spionam* is the Russian equivalent of "Death To Spies," and it is the root of the acronym SMERSH.

273) **C.**

274) **B.**

Ross Kananga is the specialist who supervised the croc and alligator scenes, and performed the stunts with those animals at the Louisiana location. Screenwriter Tom Mankiewicz appropriated Kananga's name for the identity of Mr. Big during Big's appearances as the political leader of the island nation of San Monique.

275) **A.**

He arrives at Bond's hotel all bandaged up, with a quaint note attached to his bloody wrapping. It reads, "He disagreed with something that ate him."

276) **B.**

It's also the site of the heroin refinery used by Mr. Big.

277) **C.**

It was brought over from London and sprayed a dull grayish-green color to simulate "San Monique Transport."

278) **B.**

The tarot cards used in *LIVE AND LET DIE* (some of which are pictured on the next two pages) were specially designed for Eon Productions by Scottish-born Fergus Hall. For the 78-card tarot fortune-telling deck, Mr. Hall made 42 original oil paintings, each weighing slightly over one pound and measuring 12½ inches high, 8 inches wide and ½ inch thick. The cards were manufactured at the art facilities of A.G. Muller & Cie in Switzerland, and an official "James Bond Tarot Game" was made commercially available in English, French, German, Spanish, Italian, Portuguese, Japanese and many other languages.

279) **C.**

280) **A.**

Underground, they are greeted by Mr. Big and Company. This device was obviously kept for use in the film.

281) **D.**

Bond first *tries* to bring over the rowboat with his magnetic wristwatch, but the boat is tied firmly to a tree. Instead, once the crocodiles lined up (Ross Kananga had tied their feet to the bottom of the pond), 007 runs across their backs and escapes onto dry land. (This difficult stunt was performed by Kananga, who had to wear the same kind of shoes as Bond, and as a result kept falling into the water.)

282) **D.**

However, she does say, "He brings violence and destruction."

283) **TRUE.**
She also utters some nonsense about how a bridge to a secret temple has been destroyed.

284) **A.**
He asks her to pick one card from the rigged deck, and when it comes up "Lovers," her worst fears seem justified. Of course she soon succumbs.

285) **C.**
Bond introduces the man to Rosie Carver as "the man who shares my hairbrush," calling him Quarrel, Junior. The character of Quarrel makes his first appearance in Fleming's novel *LIVE AND LET DIE,* which was written before the novel *DOCTOR NO.* Quarrel had to be given a new name, obviously, because he had died a fiery death in the movie *DOCTOR NO.*

286) **C.**
Harold Strutter

287) **C.**
Bond gets a tip from Felix Leiter regarding the registration on a "white pimp-mobile," plate number 347–NDG. It was signed out to the Oh Cult Voodoo Shop, located at 33 East 56th Street. As 007 wanders around the voodoo paraphenalia, he sees Whisper disappear through a side door, and asks the salesgirl to gift wrap a stuffed snake, length-wise.

288) **B.**

289) **B.**

290) **D.**
As the leader of San Monique, his own country, Mr. Big was, in essence, working for himself.

I'VE GROWN ACCUSTOMED TO THAT FACE

291) **B.**
He's the one who kicks Kronsteen in the leg and who is himself burned to a crisp in the climactic boat chase.

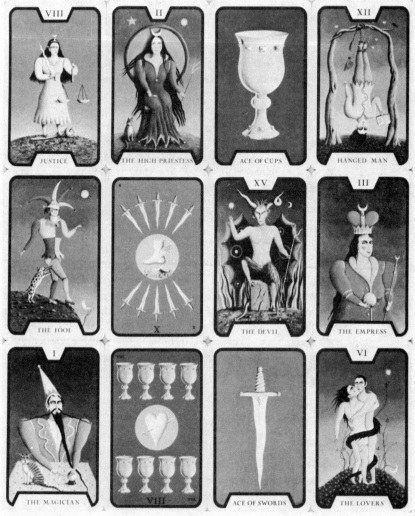

TAROT CARDS

(CREDIT: U.S. GAMES SYSTEMS, INC.)

292) **FALSE.**

In *DOCTOR NO,* the role of the Armorer was played by Peter Burton, and in *LIVE AND LET DIE,* Llewelyn was busy doing an English television show called "Folleyfoot" and couldn't leave the country to join Bond in New Orleans.

293) **A.**

In *YOU ONLY LIVE TWICE,* Rimmer is the Mission Control radar operator who has to call Houston to say he's lost the spacecraft from his scope. In *DIAMONDS ARE FOREVER,* he's one of the technicians at Whyte Techtronics. Mr. Rimmer always seems to pop up as the American in British-made films, including the Superman and Charlie Muffin.

294) **A.**

He's also known as Frederick Gray.

295) **B.**

296) **B.**

Miss Beswick appears as Paula Caplan in *THUNDERBALL,* a woman who decides to kill herself rather than talk.

297) **A–1, B–5, C–4, D–3, E–2, F–6**

Jack Lord, who went on to fame in such television shows as "Stoney Burke" and "Hawaii Five-O," played Felix Leiter in *DOCTOR NO.* Interestingly enough, not only is the Leiter character *not* in the Fleming novel of *DOCTOR NO,* but he doesn't even resemble Lord. In Fleming's second book, *LIVE AND LET DIE,* Leiter falls prey to a hungry shark. But the shark doesn't like the taste of CIA men, and spits him back out, causing the *yellow-*haired Leiter to hobble about with a wooden leg and steel claw throughout the remaining novels.

David Hedison, the first (and so far only) Leiter to play with Roger Moore's Bond, has played Captain Lee Crane on television's "Voyage to the Bottom of the Sea," and has appeared in the CBS movie *THE GAMBLER,* as well as the 12-hour NBC miniseries "A.D."

Bernie Casey is the first black actor to portray the character. Casey is a former L.A. Ram and San Francisco Forty-Niner, who's appeared in *THE MAN WHO FELL TO EARTH* and *SHARKEY'S MACHINE.*

298) **B.**

Until his death, Bernard Lee played "M" in every Bond film from *DOCTOR NO* to *MOONRAKER.*

299) **A–8, B–3, C–6, D–5, E–1, F–2, G–4, H–7**
George Baker played Sir Hilary Bray and Captain Benson; Robert Brown played Admiral Hargreaves and "M"; Bert Kwok played Mr. Ling and SPECTRE headman #3; Marc Lawrence played Rodney and the thug who tossed Plenty O'Toole out the window; Nadja Regin played Bonita and Kerim's whining girlfriend; Angela Scoular played Ruby and Buttercup; Lizzie Warville played Gogol's Russian girl friend and one of the "Bond Beauties"; and Alison Worth was a "Bond Beauty" and one of the "Octopussies."

300) **A.**
He's Dikko Henderson in *YOU ONLY LIVE TWICE*.

THE MAN WITH THE GOLDEN GUN

301) **B.**
Bond had lost his memory after killing Blofeld in the novel of *YOU ONLY LIVE TWICE*. He was always on the verge of some kind of emotional collapse, and his sorrow over the death of his nemesis, compounded by the physical demands of the mission, left him a shell of his former self. He was presumed dead—in fact, "M" had already written an obituary of him for the London *Times*. But during the period of his convalesence with Kissy Suzuki in Japan, Bond recognizes certain things. The word "Vladivostock" means something to him; he isn't sure what. At the end of *YOU ONLY LIVE TWICE*, 007 heads for that Russian port city, and subsequently, in *THE MAN WITH THE GOLDEN GUN*, he returns to London with a cyanide gun to kill "M." It becomes apparent to both "M" and Chief-of-Staff Bill Tanner that 007 has been brainwashed and needs help.

302) **B.**

303) **C.**

304) **D.**

305) **TRUE.**
She invites 007 for a swim, at which point he takes off his shirt to reveal a fake third nipple. This obvious fake is a ploy to get people to believe he's really "The Man With The Golden Gun" himself.

306) **A.**

Bond travels to Cairo in search of clues to the death of 002 when he spots a golden bullet in the bellybutton of a belly dancer. He tries to get it from her, and accidently swallows it as a fight breaks out. The distraught young lady exclaims, after the bullet has been freed from her bellybutton, "I've lost my charm!" 007 voices his disagreement.

307) **FALSE.**

While Bond believes it is the body of Mary Goodnight at the time, he soon finds out that Scaramanga used a dummy to scare the living daylights out of him.

308) **B.**

309) **C.**

She even manages to catch a few winks while Bond and Andrea entertain one another.

310) **B.**

Lieutenant Hip doesn't identify himself as working with the British Secret Service because he doesn't know how much 007 knows about the mission.

311) **TRUE.**

During the boat chase, Bond's boat slows down and comes to a halt. He's trying to figure out what's gone wrong, when a local boy selling souvenirs jumps aboard, saying that he'll fix it. 007 says he'll pay him if he does. The lad merely flips a switch and the boat starts right up. When the boy demands payment, Bond tosses him overboard.

312) **C.**

Used in conjunction with other equipment, the system converts the rays of the sun into useful energy.

313) **A.**

Lieutenant Hip doesn't mention that his two young nieces are quite capable of handling themselves, thank you. But when the fight begins, he informs Bond that their father owns a karate school. The two girls proceed to subdue an entire battalion.

314) **D.**

315) **D.**

Even for the most ardent Bond fans, the fact that 007 is wearing the same costume that Scaramanga has chosen to outfit the practice dummy in does strain the film's credibility.

316) **FALSE.**

Hai Fat is not convinced, especially considering the fact that he was just talking to the real Scaramanga when Bond arrived.

317) **A.**

What J.W. Pepper, an American tourist on holiday, is doing in an American Motors dealership in the middle of Bangkok shall forever remain a cinematic mystery.

318) **D.**

Bond is trying to unscrew the covering that houses the agitator when Goodnight's butt hits a switch that turns on the solar energy gatherer. By the hair of his head, Bond avoids getting roasted alive.

319) **TRUE.**

Bond had never been offered a knighthood before, but he does not wish to become a titled citizen after all he's been through. Of Scottish parentage (at least his father was a Scot), Bond feels he should be loyal to his heritage.

320) **A.**

Raised in a circus, Scaramanga's pet elephant "Max" was accidentally shot. The young and impressionable boy was greatly disturbed by this and shot the man who killed his animal. The story is used in different forms in the novel and the movie. (AUTHOR'S NOTE: Christopher Lee, the man who played Scaramanga, was a distant relative of Ian Fleming's, and was actually one of the late author's "role models" for the character of Doctor No. Note, too, that Lee ended up playing quite a different character in another Ian Fleming story.)

THAT'S WHY THEY CALL IT THE BOOB TUBE

321) **B.**

It was for the third installment of the CBS television series "Climax," and it aired on Thursday, October 21, from 8:30 to 9:30 P.M. Barry Nelson played an American 007 in a one-hour adaptation of *CASINO ROYALE* written by Anthony Ellis. Peter Lorre portrayed Le Chiffre, and Linda Christian played Bond's former girl friend, Valerie Mathis. According to film historian Jim Shoenberger, the show was divided into three acts (and the actors made quite a few mistakes during this live show). In the show —not the book—Valerie, Bond's love interest, was Le Chiffre's mistress. According to Shoenberger, "The story highlights are the desperate game of *baccarat* between the two adversaries, a surprisingly savage torture scene for live television, and the final battle to the death between Bond, Le Chiffre and his henchmen." The associate producer was Elliot Louis, the executive producer was Ben Feiner, Jr., and the show was directed by William H. Brown, Jr.

322) **C.**

In the television outline, American rockets are being tampered with and Gunn is sent to find out what's happening. When the television project fell through, Fleming adapted the discarded story for his own book, *DOCTOR NO*. Fleming made a habit of using discarded material, and turned a few script outlines for a James Bond television series into the novel *FOR YOUR EYES ONLY*. However, when he tried turning the *THUNDERBALL* script into a novel (once it seemed that the movie project was dead) he got into a little more trouble than he bargained for, and the authorship and ownership of that story wound up being decided in the British courts.

323) **B.**

GOLDFINGER had a 49 percent share of the viewing audience the night it was first aired on an American network. *FROM RUSSIA WITH LOVE, THUNDERBALL* and *LIVE AND LET DIE* each racked up a 40 percent share or better, and *DIAMONDS ARE FOREVER, DOCTOR NO* and *YOU ONLY LIVE TWICE* each notched a 37 percent share. In other markets, some of the Bond films have been aired as many as 18 times, establishing top-ten ratings virtually every time. When eleven of the James Bond films were sold to RCA for the rights to put them on Selectavision videodisc, close to two million dollars was reportedly paid to United Artists and Eon Productions for the rights to the whole bunch.

324) **C.**

Based on an examination of the average number of subscribers who tune in to view HBO programming, the James Bond films generally receive twice the average viewership. *THE SPY WHO LOVED ME* is virtually tied with *FOR YOUR EYES ONLY* as the most popular film on the cable network, with the "tune-in" edge leaning towards *THE SPY WHO LOVED ME*. Also on Home Box Office, viewers can rate how they like a certain "product" via a measurement something called the "satisfaction dimension." According to this guideline, the James Bond films get between 25 and 30 percent higher marks for "viewer satisfaction" than the typical HBO product. So it seems that the moviegoers sitting at home want the original, uncut versions of the James Bond films, and will watch them time and time again.

325) A.

On October 28, 1975, *DOCTOR NO* was viewed by approximately 51 percent of the available viewing audience in Great Britain. This means that some 10 million British television viewers watched at least a portion of the movie. While *DOCTOR NO* received the highest TVR rating, *THE SPY WHO LOVED ME* achieved the largest numerical audience, with well over 22 million viewers tuning in to watch at least a scene or two on March 28, 1982. (Forty-five percent of the available viewing audience contributed to this figure, earning *SPY* the second-highest audience rating for the Bond films in Britain).

Other statistics provided by the IBA indicate that James Bond is only slightly more popular with men than women, although *DOCTOR NO, LIVE AND LET DIE* and *THE MAN WITH THE GOLDEN GUN* seem a bit more popular with the ladies.

FROM RUSSIA WITH LOVE was most popular with adults over 55 years old; *FROM RUSSIA WITH LOVE* and *YOU ONLY LIVE TWICE* tied for the affections of the 35- to 54-year-olds, and *YOU ONLY LIVE TWICE* won the hearts of 16- to 34-year-olds.

THE SPY WHO LOVED ME

326) B.

Sergei Borzov was Anya Amasova's lover. Agent Triple X was Anya herself.

327) A.

Berngarten, in the Austrian Alps.

328) A.

Also known as the "Love Theme" from *DOCTOR ZHIVAGO*.

329) **FALSE.**

Bond and Anya are aboard a barge floating down the Nile towards Cairo when she blows sleep dust at him through a specially-crafted KGB cigarette.

330) **A, B and C.**

Bond orders a Baccardi on the rocks for Anya, and she returns the favor by ordering him a vodka martini, shaken not stirred. She goes on to say he was recruited from the Royal Navy, that he's had many lady friends, and that his wife was killed—at which point 007 interrupts her, admitting he is sensitive about certain topics.

331) **TRUE.**

He also stipulated in his deal with Eon Productions that, should they ever decide to make a film version of *THE SPY WHO LOVED ME,* they would retain only the title. Apparently, even back in 1962, Fleming realized that his attempt to write a Bond adventure from a female point of view had not succeeded. In the novel, 007 doesn't arrive until page 90, after we've learned more than we care to about the hapless Vivienne Michel.

332) **B.**

333) **A.**

334) **C.**

335) **B.**

336) **B.**

Their full names are Sluggsy Morant and Sol Horowitz. Phancey is the name of the motel manager, Sanguinetti is the owner of the place. Morrow and O'Donnell are the names of the police detectives who arrive the morning after Vivienne's night of terror. The characters in answer "C" do not appear in *THE SPY WHO LOVED ME.*

337) **D.**

Horst Uhlman is the name of an ex-Gestapo agent and a current member of SPECTRE. Uhlman is sent to Canada to kill a Russian defector. (renamed Boris for security purposes.) Uhlman was going to be paid for

Boris's death, but Uhlman himself is shot and killed by a Canadian Mountie.

338) **D.**

Naomi, played by Caroline Munro, was one of Stromberg's operatives, and in her helicopter, she followed Bond's Lotus to the dock and into the water. While she waited to make sure 007 was dead, she was killed and the helicopter was destroyed by 007's missile.

339) **A.**

This same actor appears in *MOONRAKER*, when Bond drives his motorized gondola around St. Mark's Square, and again during the exciting ski chase in *FOR YOUR EYES ONLY*. It is rumored that he is a personal friend of producer Broccoli.

340) **C.**

341) **D.**

Sandor, played by Milton Reid, and Jaws, played by Richard Kiel

342) **FALSE.**

Stromberg is not interested in extortion—in fact, he doesn't really want anything from anybody. All he wants is to fulfill his dream of a new civilization underwater, which, unfortunately for the rest of the world, can only be achieved by setting off World War Three.

343) **A.**

While it is highly unlikely that the head of the British Secret Service and the head of the Russian KGB would be on such friendly terms, it seems both "M" and Gogol act like old chums as they walk through to "Q" branch. Upon reaching a narrow doorway, "M" says, "After you, Alexis," to which Gogol replies, "No, no, no. After you, Miles." This is a charming but uncharacteristic exchange, when one considers that it was Fleming who always made such a big deal about the absolute secrecy surrounding "M" 's true identity. Ah, detente.

344) **B.**

If the "impulse conductor circuit" is allowed to touch the conductor, Bond would blow up everyone, including himself (believe it or not!). But everything goes okay and 007 sets the fuse for 20 seconds. The bomb works, and the battle rages on inside the *Leparus*.

345) **FALSE.**
Admiral Hargreaves isn't there.

IF YOU HUM A FEW BARS, I THINK I CAN FAKE IT

346) **C.**

347) **A.**
The "Lawrence Of Arabia" theme was played during Bond and Anya's walk through the desert in *THE SPY WHO LOVED ME.*

348) **D.**

349) **B.**
It is also sometimes referred to as the theme from the movie *ELVIRA MADIGAN.*

350) **FALSE.**
According to *THE FILMS OF JAMES BOND* by Stephen Jay Rubin, John Barry wrote the two-and-a-half-minute theme that became world famous. Barry's orchestra played the theme song in *DOCTOR NO,* and according to the story, he wrote the song without ever having seen the film.

351) **C.**
Herb Alpert and the Tijuana Brass performed the theme for *CASINO ROYALE,* Tom Jones performed the theme from *THUNDERBALL,* and Carly Simon sang "Nobody Does It Better" for *THE SPY WHO LOVED ME.*

352) **D.**

353) **A–12, B–9, C–1, D–3, E–10, F–8, G–5, H–4, I–2, J–7, K–11, L–6**
"All Time High" was the theme from *OCTOPUSSY,* "Do You Know How Christmas Trees Are Grown" was from *ON HER MAJESTY'S SECRET SERVICE,* "The Look Of Love" was from *CASINO ROYALE* and "Make It Last All Night" was from *FOR YOUR EYES ONLY.*

354) **C.**
"Goldfinger," "Diamonds Are Forever" and "Moonraker." The "Goldfinger" theme is somewhat different on the record album than in

the movie, and for *MOONRAKER,* Miss Bassey sang two versions; one a slower title tune, and the closing, disco-sounding end theme.

355) **FALSE.**

Not one of the hit songs from a James Bond movie has ever won an Academy Award for Best Original Song.

MOONRAKER

356) **TRUE.**

357) **C.**

The name of her betrothed is Detective-Inspector Vivian, and the wedding is set for Saturday, the day after the mission is to be finished.

358) **D.**

Before the war (World War Two), Esposito taught Bond all sorts of card tricks—the "Rifle Stack," how to deal "Seconds and Bottoms and Middles," how to wax the aces and how do a whole array of assorted card chicanery.

359) **B.**

007 grabs the pilot as they fall to the earth. But soon there is a fight for the parachute, and Bond manages to take it away from the poor fellow.

360) **B.**

361) **C.**

Later in the movie, when Bond and Holly are on their way to Drax's space station, 007 notices the cargo in his shuttle: 6 men and 6 women. Simple arithmetic will tell you that if there are 6 space shuttles, 72 astronauts were probably being trained for Drax's space breeding farm.

362) **A.**

363) **B.**

One of Drax's henchmen, Chang, had seen Corrine assist Bond with the safe, and apparently informed his master. The very next day, when her services are no longer required, a pack of hungry dogs is sent scurrying after her through Drax's private forest. As the hounds settle in for a feast of French brunette, the camera tilts up and away.

364) **C.**
Bond is about to pass out when he suddenly recalls the time he first tested his specially-equipped wristwatch in "M"'s office. Firing one of its armor piercing heads causes a malfunction in the centrifuge, and 007 is lucky to remain alive. (NOTE: As far as I know, this is the only time a flashback is used in the entire Bond series.)

365) **FALSE.**
The tantalizingly brief snug white outfit that appears in the poster advertisement never actually appears on Ms. Chiles in the film. White uniforms are worn by Drax's personal staff of astronauts.

366) **A.**

367) **A.**
An exciting battle ensues high over the beautiful city of Rio de Janiero. Bond and Holly are able to escape by sliding down the cable with the aid of a chain. Jaws has quite a different trip down.

368) **B.**
The character's name is Dolly, and she is played by French actress Blanche Ravalec. During the sequence, Jaws does lift a large device off himself, and there are certainly enough plugs for "7-Up" scattered across the location to make even the staunchest cola fan run to the concession stand.

369) **B.**
According to the novel *THE SPY WHO LOVED ME* by Christopher Wood, Jaws was born in Poland, the product of a union between a circus strongman and a prison wardress. He played basketball in school, and was beaten by Polish Police when he was suspected to have been a participant in the bread riots of 1972. The police destroyed his entire mouth and left him for dead, but Jaws isn't a quitter (as you may have noticed). After meeting Mr. Stromberg (see *THE SPY WHO LOVED ME*), his mouth was repaired with steel. To enable him to operate the steel jaw, his vocal chords had to be severed, turning him into a rather unusual looking mute. (It's surprising, therefore, when, in *MOON-RAKER*, he actually speaks.)

370) **B.**

371) **C.**

372) **B.**

373) **A.**
But Drax had other ideas in mind, and specifically designed the Moonraker rocket to strike the unsuspecting city of London.

374) **C.**
Bond shoots him with a cyanide dart from that fabulous wristwatch gizmo, and pushes Hugo Drax out through an airlock into space.

375) **D.**
Although "Q" says that he thinks Bond is attempting re-entry, the line is uttered in response to "M"'s question, "What the devil does Bond think he's doing?" With a wonderful smile, Holly does ask Bond to take her around the world again, to which the intrepid 007 responds, "Why not?"

FAMOUS LAST WORDS

376) **D.**

377) **B.**

378) **B.**
Patricia is the nurse at Shrublands in *THUNDERBALL* who is at first unmoved by 007's charms, but ultimately is sorry to see him leave.

379) **C.**

380) **C.**
Mr. Reagan appeared with dozens of other international personalities on a program called "James Bond: The First 21 Years." The President made the remark for the show that was originally slated for broadcast in the United Kingdom only. A minor stir was caused when station WTTG-TV in Washington used the President's filmed excerpt to promote the upcoming broadcast of the show on the station. Among his other remarks, Mr.

Reagan added that the fictitious British agent was "fearless, skilled, courageous, optimistic and one other thing: he always gets his girl."

381) **C.**
This is also the name of the last chapter in the novel, and refers to the ironic situation presented by Tracy's sudden death.

382) **B.**

383) **A.**
Through Miss Moneypenny's machinations, 007's request for resignation turns into merely two weeks leave, satisfying both Bond and "M."

384) **B.**
This was the description entered into courtroom proceedings by attorneys for Kevin McClory. A description of James Bond was needed during the trial to determine who owned the rights to *THUNDERBALL,* and this is the one supplied by the attorneys who were trying to pursuade Justice Sir Lynn Ungoed-Thomas that their client was entitled to some credit for his work on the story.

385) **B.**
Charles K. Feldman, producer and "maven" behind the making of "Little Cleopatra," otherwise known as *CASINO ROYALE*

FOR YOUR EYES ONLY

386) **C.**

387) **B.**
The full inscription on the stone read: "Theresa Bond. 1943–1969. Beloved wife of James Bond. We have all the time in the world."

388) **B.**

389) **B.**
His name is Hector Gonzales, and he is played by Stephan Kalipha. The Gonzales character first appeared in the short story *FOR YOUR EYES ONLY* as the man responsible for the death of the Havelocks.

390) B.

She had previously appeared in Luis Bunuel's film *THAT OBSCURE OBJECT OF DESIRE*. During production, the 23-year-old green-eyed beauty gave an interview in which she said of co-star Roger Moore: "He's very nice. He reminds me of my father." She was the only major star of the film absent from the American press tour.

391) A.

Bond and Solitaire are to be dragged behind Mr. Big's yacht until shredded by sea coral and eaten by sharks. Kristatos seems to have read Fleming.

392) C.

393) D.

The A.T.A.C. worked on an ultra-low frequency to communicate launching instructions to British submarines for their Polaris missiles.

394) D.

395) A.

"Operation Extase" was the name given Bond's assignment for the Fleming short story "The Living Daylights."

396) B.

Bond plans to, Melina tries to, but Columbo is the one who succeeds in killing his arch enemy high atop the Meteora peak, in what's called "St. Cyrils."

397) B.

Luigi Ferrara is Bond's contact in Northern Italy. He introduces 007 to Aris Kristatos, but is killed in Bond's car outside the ice hockey practice rink. Apostis is the man who tries killing Bond as ol' Jimmy climbs up the side of the mountain towards the end of the film. Eric Kriegler is the Olympic skier who works for the Russians and tries killing Bond along the slopes and bobsled run.

398) D.

In the July 1979 issue of *Playboy,* potential entrants were asked to send in two photographs of themselves—one a face shot, one a full-figured swimsuit shot, along with a description in 50 words or less of why they felt they belonged in the next James Bond film. Robin was modeling in Fort Lauderdale when she entered the contest. Three months later she learned she had become a semi-finalist, and then the field was narrowed down to three for a screen test to be shot in California. Albert Broccoli, director Lewis Gilbert, Roger Moore and Hugh M. Hefner were all supposed to judge the final screen tests. Robin was finally cast in the part of the florist shop attendant, and was used during the sequences shot in Cortina.

399) **C.**
After the story is over, Colombo gives 007 the keys to Lisl's room as a gift.

400) **A.**
The Neptune is a two-man "lockout" sub, and when Melina and 007 are beneath the water ready to return to the surface, a tiny one-man Osel submersible unleashes a deadly attack on them. Just before they returned to the sub, Bond and Melina fought a deadly battle with a man in a large, white "JIM" underwater diving suit. 007 dispatches the diver by placing a limpet mine on the back of the suit, turning the intruder into sea pulp.

401) **TRUE.**
This happens while Bond is playing *baccarat* in the casino at Corfu. Playing with a man named Bunky, 007 turns up what appears on the screen to merely be a five. The croupier turns Bunky's cards over to reveal an eight, but says *"neuf a la banque"* on behalf of James Bond's obviously weaker cards, giving Bond the benefit of a hand of nine and a win.

402) **A.**
The Israeli-born actor, whose full name is Chaim Topol, played Tevye the milkman both on the London stage and in the United Artists film presentation of the musical *FIDDLER ON THE ROOF*.

403) **D.**
Bond tosses the A.T.A.C. over the cliff, where it tumbles to the ground, exploding in a million pieces. Calling it another aspect of detente, 007 says "You don't have it. I don't have it."

404) **D.**
At Indiana University in Bloomington, the Lilly Library houses the collection of most of Ian Fleming's original manuscripts. It also has the

collected papers from two authors who were preparing biographies on the late author. In that collection can be found the original titles to some of Fleming's other works. For instance, *LIVE AND LET DIE* was originally titled *The Undertaker's Wind, MOONRAKER* was originally called *Mondays Are Hell, GOLDFINGER* was originally called *The Richest Man In The World,* and *ON HER MAJESTY'S SECRET SERVICE* was called *The Belles of Hell.* For a more detailed account of the Lilly Collection the library suggests consulting an issue of the James Bond Fan Club magazine, *Bondage,* no. 12, 1983.

405) **A.**

In the story, "M" had been best man at the Havelocks' wedding on Malta back in 1925, and when they were ruthlessly killed because they did not wish to sell their home and property to von Hammerstein, "M" feels that justice must be served, so he turns to his own licensed-to-kill operative.

I'LL TAKE ODDS AND ENDS FOR $20

406) **B.**

First spotted by producer Harry Saltzman in an aviation magazine, the miniature autogiro was invented by Wing Commander Ken Wallis, who flew "Little Nellie" for the cameras, doubling for Sean Connery. Based on the Beagle-Wallis WA-116, this steel and fiberglass contraption has forward firing machine guns, rockets, rear-ejection flamethrowers, air-to-air missiles and "underchutes with explosives attached." It was delivered to Bond in Japan by "Q," and came conveniently unassembled in four suitcases. Box number one held the engine and tools for assembling it, box number two contained some wrenches, the control panel and part of the tubular steel frame, box number three contained the rest of the framing structure, and box number four housed the propeller, hinged rotor blades and tailpiece.

407) **B.**

Jaws is a completely original character created solely by the makers of the Bond films. He has nothing whatsoever to do with anything Ian Fleming ever wrote. Producer Broccoli claims credit for the creation, saying that after meeting the actor Richard Kiel in America, he returned to London and told the writers to come up with something for the 7'2" actor. Christopher Wood gave the character a past (see answer 369).

408) **C.**

While Willard Whyte's life in *DIAMONDS ARE FOREVER* clearly resembles that of the former recluse (a millionaire living on top of a Las Vegas hotel who hasn't been seen in public for years), Broccoli has said he got the idea for *THE SPY WHO LOVED ME* from an operation that involved Howard Hughes and the CIA. According to public statements, the Hughes corporation had built an enormous deep-sea vessel named *The Glomar Explorer.* Its apparent function was to mine the ocean bottom off the coast of Hawaii for mineral deposits, but in fact the real mission was part of a CIA-subsidized project called Jennifer, and the *Glomar*'s mission was to retrieve a sunken Soviet nuclear submarine. The project was a closely kept secret during the Nixon and Ford administrations, and only became public after press reports leaked it in 1975. As for *DIAMONDS ARE FOREVER,* producer Broccoli admits he and Howard Hughes were friends, and one night he had a dream wherein Hughes was actually being held hostage by others who ran his empire. This was the start of *DIAMONDS ARE FOREVER.*

409) **FALSE.**

No Bond book has ever been legally published within the Soviet Union. At the time of its original publication, however, *DOCTOR NO* was excerpted in *Izvestia,* the Moscow daily. The paper went on to say, "Fleming prides himself on his knowledge of espionage and villainy. His best friend is Allen Dulles, former head of the U.S. Central Intelligence Agency, who even attempted (but unsuccessfully) to try methods recommended by Fleming in his books. Obviously American propagandists must be in a bad way if they have recourse to the help of an English retired spy turned mediocre writer." Those Russians sure have a way of phrasing things.

410) **C.**

Mr. Broccoli has been married to his third wife, novelist Dana Wilson, since 1959. They have four children, one of whom is Mr. Wilson, a former New York attorney who has been involved with Eon Productions since 1972. He was assistant to the producer on *THE SPY WHO LOVED ME,* executive producer on *MOONRAKER,* and executive producer and co-screenwriter on *FOR YOUR EYES ONLY* and *OCTOPUSSY.*

411) **FALSE.**

Columbia Pictures was one of the studios that had turned down the chance to do the James Bond films back in the late 1950s–early 1960s.

When Harry Saltzman decided it was time to sell out his interest in the James Bond money machine, he offered to sell to Columbia. But United Artists, who along with Eon Productions actually has a financial share as producer of the films, apparently did not wish to just hand over instant money to Columbia the competitor, so they bought up Saltzman and are now partners with Broccoli in the making of the Bond movies.

412) **B.**

Geoffrey Boothroyd was a weapons enthusiast, and beginning in 1956 he and Ian Fleming began a correspondence concerning 007's guns and holsters. In recognition and appreciation for his help and guidance, Fleming named the Armorer from "Q" branch Major Boothroyd. He was called that in the film *DOCTOR NO*, but since Mr. Llewelyn has played the role, the part is listed—and has become famous—as "Q." Llewelyn insists that his name is simply "Q" and that he's not Boothroyd. But in *THE SPY WHO LOVED ME*, Anya can clearly be heard calling him Major Boothroyd.

413) **C.**

1964–*GOLDFINGER:* winner, best Sound Effects (Norman Wanstall)
1965–*THUNDERBALL:* winner; best Special Visual Effects (John Stears)
   Other nominations that were received but did not win:
1967–*CASINO ROYALE:* music nomination for "The Look Of Love" (music and lyrics by Burt Bacharach and Hal David)
1971–*DIAMONDS ARE FOREVER:* nomination for best sound (Gordon K. McCallum, John Mitchell and Alfred J. Overton)
1973–*LIVE AND LET DIE:* nomination for original song "Live And Let Die" (music and lyrics by Paul and Linda McCartney)
1977–*THE SPY WHO LOVED ME:* nomination for art direction (Ken Adam, Peter Lamont, Hugh Scaife), nomination for original score (Marvin Hamlisch), nomination for original song (music by Marvin Hamlisch, lyrics by Carole Bayer Sager)
1979–*MOONRAKER:* nomination for visual effects (Derek Meddings, Paul Wilson, John Evans)
1981–*FOR YOUR EYES ONLY:* nomination for original song "For Your Eyes Only" (music by Bill Conti, lyrics by Michael Leeson)
   In 1981, the Irving G. Thalberg Memorial Award was given to producer Albert R. Broccoli for continued excellence in the quality of his James Bond films.

414) **B.**

Baccarat and *chemin de fer* became popular in French casinos during the 1830s. There are many similarities in the two games, and because of the widespread popularity of both games around the world, what may be called *baccarat* in one casino may more nearly represent *chemin de fer* in another. In *chemin de fer*, six decks of cards are generally used, although there can be eight decks. The shoe (card container) is reshuffled when approximately five-sixths of the deck has been used. In *baccarat*, three decks are generally used, but in the United States, something often called "baccarat–chemin de fer" requires six to eight standard decks of cards. Basically, the game is similar to black jack, with each player drawing cards in an attempt to approach the value 9 but not exceed it. Picture cards have no face value, and anything over a 9 automatically loses 10 points; for example, a five and a seven, rather than becoming the value 12, becomes the value 2—not a good hand at all.

415) **C.**

When Mie Hama came down with heat prostration while shooting on location in Japan, Connery's blonde wife donned a black wig, almond-shaped her eyes and did the underwater scenes for Miss Hama.

416) **B.**

The Shark Hunter II was employed by Stromberg's men, and was used during the underwater chase involving Bond, Anya and the Lotus Esprit.

417) **D.**

During the days when Fleming had been trying to get a television development deal, a producer for a U.S. television network approached him with the idea for an "intelligent" superspy stationed in New York. Fleming did not work on the project, but did jot down some notes for the producer, among which were the names Napoleon Solo and April Dancer. These characters were later used in the series "The Man From U.N.C.L.E." The character of Solo, used in *GOLDFINGER*, was nothing more than a two-bit hoodlum, and in no way resembled the suave Napoleon of the TV series.

418) **FALSE.**

The James Bond 007 Fan Club, which was started in 1974 by two teenagers from Yonkers, is run by president Richard Schenkman, along with the help of anyone who's interested. The club has members in over 20 countries around the world (there are currently over 2,000 members), who receive two copies of the fan club magazine and two newsletters every year. The average age of the members in the club is 25, and it is entirely supported by membership dues and merchandising under the supervision of Mr. Schenkman.

419) **A.**
In fact it is the name of the fan club magazine. Interviews in the pages of *Bondage* have included such Bond personalities as Albert R. Broccoli, Roger Moore, Tom Mankiewicz, Terence Young, George Lazenby, Derek Meddings, Bob Simmons and Kevin McClory.

420) **B.**
Inside the home of Vesper Lynd, the statue of Lord Nelson from London's Trafalgar Square sits quietly in bold light. Wolf Mankowitz, who contributed to the original *DOCTOR NO* script before bowing out, was one of the writers on *CASINO ROYALE,* so it would seem that this is his touch.

OCTOPUSSY

421) **B.**
Herr Oberhauser supposedly guided Smythe through the Alps in order to find the location of a Nazi treasure hoard. When Smythe found the gold, he killed Oberhauser so that no one would know who discovered this Nazi wealth. James Bond, it seems, knew Oberhauser as a youth and, according to James himself, was taught how to ski by the Swiss native during Bond's childhood.

422) **B.**
Fleming wanted his readers to feel that when Bond, left Smythe by himself for a short while Smythe might do the honorable thing and kill himself, rather than return to London to face the inevitable inquiry and jail sentence. When Smythe goes out to his pet "octopussy instead," his death wish is granted.

423) **C.**
"The Property of a Lady" was a story involving a Fabergé Egg and an auction at Sotheby's.

424) **B.**

425) **A.**

Mr. Fornof is the owner and pilot of the AcroJet, of which there are only two in existance in the world. It is capable of speeds around 310 m.p.h and can climb at a rate of 2,800 feet per minute. According to Michael Wilson, the AcroJet was actually written in the script for *MOON-RAKER,* but was later taken out—and saved for a rainy day.

426) **D.**

The model for the Fabergé Egg used in *OCTOPUSSY* was an Imperial Easter Egg, also known as the Coronation Egg, and was created for Tsar Nicholas II in 1897. Within the egg itself is a replica of the imperial coach used at the Nicholas and Alexandra Coronation.

427) **C.**

428) **B.**

Ms. Wayborn is a Swedish track champion, and has been a race car driver, a jockey, a horse trainer, a wild animal trainer, a clothing designer, and is interested in gourmet cooking. She has appeared as Greta Garbo in the TV movie *GARBO,* and her dramatic exit from 007's bedroom in *OCTOPUSSY* certainly must rank up there with one of moviedom's more memorable exeunts.

429) **D.**

With the help of "Q," Bond has planted a homing device inside the egg and knows he'll be able to follow it to whoever killed Agent 009 in Berlin.

430) **B.**

Vijay was played by Vijay Amritraj, the Indian Davis Cup tennis star. In the movie, he masquerades as the local tennis pro at 007's hotel.

431) **D.**

Originally built to house the Princes of Mewar during the heavy monsoon seasons, the palace, situated high atop Lake Pichola, belonged to Bagwat Singh, the current Maharajah of Udaipur. While the exteriors of the Palace appear in long shots during the film, all the scenes involving action both inside and outside the palace were shot at Pinewood Studios, and were designed by Peter Lamont.

432) **A.**

433) **B.**

434) **D.**

435) **D.**

436) **B, C and D are all correct.**
Orlov is a madman who believes an accidental nuclear explosion on an American base in Europe will add fuel to the fires of nuclear disarmament. With Western Europe weakened, he plans to march his Soviet tanks right across the map, without fear of significant reprisal. During a boisterous meeting in the Kremlin, he tries to teach the old party bosses that this is the way a war can be waged and won in 1983, and he intends to show them how to do it.

437) **C.**
Although Smythe didn't have a child in the short story, it appears that in the movie Octopussy was his offspring. She is glad fate brought her and Bond together, so she could thank him for allowing her father the honorable alternative to imprisonment and public disgrace—suicide. This is similar to the basic idea in the short story "Octopussy," but certain facts were changed for the movie. (In the film version, Smythe had stolen a cache of Chinese gold during the Korean War, murdering a guide to conceal his own theft.)

438) **B.**

439) **B.**

440) **D.**
He has plates for the British pound.

YOU'RE GOING OUT THERE A NOBODY, BUT YOU'RE COMING BACK A STAR . . .

441) **FALSE.**
Thomas Sean Connery was born in 1930, the son of a Scottish truck driver. Roger Moore was born in 1927, the son of a British policeman.

442) **D.**

Albert R. Broccoli was once an agent who represented Miss Turner, Sean Connery appeared opposite her in the 1958 film *ANOTHER TIME, ANOTHER PLACE,* and Roger Moore starred with her in the 1955 film *DIANE.*

443) **C.**

He also indicated his love of changing diapers and preparing meals for his family. At the time, he could be seen arriving at the studio in an old Volkswagen.

444) **C.**

Besides Ms. Maxwell, Moore also met stuntman Bob Simmons when both were just starting out in the business. Simmons eventually met Cubby Broccoli back in 1952 when he was hired as a stuntman for Warwick Productions' *THE RED BERET* starring Alan Ladd. Broccoli gave Simmons other work, and he's been a part of 11 James Bond films to date.

445) **D.**

All of these men were at one time considered for the role, but John Gavin came the closest to being signed. Currently the U.S. Ambassador to Mexico, Gavin was once again under consideration to star in *DIAMONDS ARE FOREVER,* until United Artists was able to lure Sean Connery back one more time.

446) **B.**

Geoffrey Holder played Baron Samedi in *LIVE AND LET DIE.* He's also a Broadway director *(The Wiz),* choreographer *(Timbuktu)* and laughing spokesperson for the "7-Up" TV commercials.

447) **A.**

FROM RUSSIA WITH LOVE director Terence Young shot most of Armendariz's scenes as Kerim Bey without Connery at the start of shooting. After Armendariz completed the picture, he smuggled a shotgun into his hospital room and killed himself.

448) **A.**

Honey Rider is coming out of the sea singing "Underneath The Mango Tree," and Bond finishes the last two lines of the lyric for her.

449) **TRUE.**

He got them when he was in the navy, and they are usually covered up with makeup during shooting of a movie.

450) **D.**

NEVER SAY NEVER AGAIN

451) **B.**

In 1959, Fleming was introduced to Kevin McClory by mutual friends, and soon a writing partnership was under way. A feature film story was outlined dealing with James Bond and stolen atomic bombs. McClory was a film producer at the time, and brought in another writer named Jack Whittingham to punch up Fleming's dry dialogue. Whittingham and McClory, along with Fleming, developed outlines for about ten stories, most of which were discarded when they finally finished a screenplay. What was originally supposed to be called "James Bond, Secret Agent" became *THUNDERBALL.* But McClory was unable to raise financing, and the project appeared dead. Fleming went to his retreat at Goldeneye and wrote a novel called *THUNDERBALL,* which was generally (but not entirely) based on the work he had written with McClory. A court battle for rights ensued, and it was finally determined that each copy of the novel *THUNDERBALL* should have some disclaimer to the effect that the novel was based on a screen treatment by Kevin McClory, Jack Whittingham and Ian Fleming. The courts also awarded McClory film rights "in consideration of certain payments to Mr. Fleming," which is why McClory owned *THUNDERBALL* and is listed as producer on that Eon Productions film.

452) **A.**

According to Connery, his decision to play the role of 007 once more was influenced by his second and current wife, Micheline (who also came up with the title for the picture). "When Jack Schwartzman came to me to ask me to do *NEVER SAY NEVER AGAIN,* Micheline encouraged me to think about it carefully. 'Why not play the role? What do you risk? After all these years it might be interesting.' The more I thought about it, the more I thought she was right. There was also a certain amount of curiosity in me about the role, having been so long away from it."

453) **D.**

SPECTRE was born back in 1959, before James Bond ever appeared in the movie *DOCTOR NO*. SPECTRE first appeared in public in the novel *THUNDERBALL*, but had been specifically created for the movie script being written for the original *THUNDERBALL* film.

454) **C.**

Although she does see Bond through her nightfinder binoculars at Shrublands, 007 does not see her.

455) **D.**

Fatima is SPECTRE's number one assassin, who "sees the act of murder as a sort of ceremony and therefore there is a certain ritual to be gone through." A native of Nicaragua, Barbara Carrera accepted this role without even seeing a script.

456) **A.**

When Bond says that a girl he met in Philly made love better than Fatima, the wounded Ms. Blush threatens to kill him and insists that his last written words attest to her superior lovemaking. Bond distracts her and shoots her with his exploding pen.

457) **D.**

Also known as Algy, he replaces Major Boothroyd in name only, serving the same function as head of "Q Branch" for *NEVER SAY NEVER AGAIN*. The other gentlemen listed as alternatives *do* appear in this film: Klaus Maria Brandauer plays Largo, Edward Fox plays "M" and Rowan Atkinson plays Nigel Small-Fawcett.

458) **B.**

Pettachi has been able to reshape his eye with the aid of drugs, and is therefore able to confuse the machine with his eye print, which apparently matches the one belonging to the President.

459) **FALSE.**

SPECTRE issues its demands via a closed-circuit broadcast to the NATO executive committee. Clutching his white cat, Blofeld demands that SPECTRE be paid a sum totaling 25 percent of the total annual oil purchases made by the nations of the world. That's certainly a large figure and has nothing to do with *THUNDERBALL*.

460) **D.**

Hard as it may be to believe, 007 doesn't take advantage of the famed *baccarat* rooms.

461) **FALSE.**

The one-thousand-franc chips were real, so the real croupiers who worked on the film were protecting valuable property.

462) **B.**

France is only used for Largo's demonstration of the game.

463) **C.**

The Tears Of Allah refers to an ancient Middle Eastern fable. According to the fable, a prophet had wept millions of tears when his beloved lady left him, bringing forth so much water that a great well was formed. This well is what's later used as the repository for one of the bombs.

464) **A.**

Its nothing more than a training exercise, reminiscent of the pre-credit sequence used in *FROM RUSSIA WITH LOVE*. Bond is supposedly stabbed one minute and forty-seven seconds after the operation begins, which is just a few seconds shorter than it took Red Grant to kill Bond's double in the earlier film.

465) **C.**

Measuring 285 feet long and 43 feet wide, it is one of the most expensive private yachts in the world. Its real name *is* "Nabila," and the owner is billionaire Adnan Khashoggi, who allowed the cast and crew aboard this luxury vessel for location shooting. It has five full decks, three elevators, a movie theatre, two saunas, a swimming pool, a discotheque, a jacuzzi, a game room, eleven guest suites and one master suite of four rooms, and a fully operational helicopter landing pad.

466) **D.**

Bond splashes his assailant with his own urine specimen, thereby causing the man to fall back and land on a test tube, which lodges deep in his back and his chest cavity.

467) **B.**

He's apologizing to Domino for their earlier meeting at the health spa.

468) **D.**

In *THUNDERBALL,* Bond drives his Aston Martin instead of the Bentley he drove in the novels.

469) **FALSE.**

Sean Connery was in London many years ago, representing Scotland in the 1950 Mr. Universe contest, when he heard about an open audition for chorus boys in a production of the musical *South Pacific.* Apparently a 48-hour crash course in dancing was enough—he was cast in the show.

470) **A–3, B–5, C–6, D–1, E–2, F–4**

Fatima Blush was also known as Number 12; Domino's last name was Pettachi, and she was the sister of the man who hijacked the nuclear weapons; Patricia (Fearing) was the woman who attended to 007 at Shrublands; Nicole was the French operative, also known as Agent 326; the lady in the Bahamas fished James Bond out of the sea and saved his life by making love to him in her own room (Ms. Leon also appears in *THE SPY WHO LOVED ME* as the hotel receptionist in Sardinia when Bond and Anya arrive seeking Stromberg); Salem was the third actress to play Miss Moneypenny—Lois Maxwell was the first and Barbara Bouchet was the second.

EXTRA ADDED BONDAGE

471) **B.**

"M" felt he and the service were honor bound to look after those who had served it well, so Bond was sent to New York on this information-giving mission.

472) **C.**

The problem was there was no reptile house in the Central Park Zoo, so the rendezvous had to be hastily rescheduled.

473) **B.**

The name of the bar was "Harry's."

474) **B.**

Although Mary Ann Russell worked in Paris, the name of the British Secret Service station was "F," not "P." Later, while Bond is about to be killed by one of the gypsies hiding underground, she shoots his assailant with a .22. Surprised to see her there, even the cool Mr. Bond can't conceal his joy at being saved.

475) **C.**

It was named after the African professor who first discovered it in 1925. It measured six inches long, was a bright pink and had black stripes crossing its spine.

476) **D.**

After a particularly argumentative night with his wife Liz and Fidele Barbey, a native of the Seychelles Islands, Krest is found dead the next morning with his "Hildebrand Rarity" stuffed down his throat. 007 is unable to determine who is actually responsible for the death.

477) **B.**

478) **B.**

At the time, Bond was obviously looking for someone who he believed would service his every need.

479) **A.**

007 does not kill the sniper—nicknamed "Trigger," as assigned. Waiting three days in a tiny room overlooking the Berlin Wall, he had built up an entire psychological history of this female Russian gunner without ever having met her. He grows somehow attached to this opposite number, and when he makes his way across the frontier into the West, rather than shooting the sniper dead, he merely fires into her room, scaring the hell out of her.

480) **D.**

"M" and the Secret Service had known Maria Freudenstein was a mole, but were purposely feeding her misinformation to be passed on and to mislead her superiors in Moscow.

481) **A.**

482) **B.**

"Robert Markham" was the pseudonym used by Kingsley Amis when he wrote this story in 1968. Colonel Sun was a renegade Chinese officer who wanted to see a major rift develop between the Russians and the West, and hoped to use Bond and "M" as the unwitting dupes in his scheme.

The story is particularly noteworthy for its interesting use of Greek locales and for the relationship created between Bond and Ariadne Alexandrov. It also features a wonderfully "Fleming" torture: a steel rod is forced through Bond's ear into his skull by the sadistic Colonel Sun.

483) **D.**
The assumption behind Pearson's biography of Bond is that he in fact existed, and that the stories written by Fleming were attempts to turn fact into fiction. Pearson contended that by turning Bond's adventures (and the man himself) into a fictional character, we could fool the Russians and everyone else into thinking he didn't exist. It's a nice idea, and the biography fills in many of the gaps between the Fleming novels.

484) **D.**

485) **D.**
Trudi Parker was renamed Corrine Dufour for the film version.

486) **C.**

487) **C.**
This is precisely what happens, and at the castle, Bond learns all about Murik's dirty deeds.

488) **C.**

489) **B.**

490) **A.**
He was still called 007 in deference to his abilities and his history. "M" wasn't at all thrilled with the notion of closing the "double 0" section, so Bond unofficially retained his number, with an official sanction from his boss.

THE JAMES BOND 007 DOSSIER QUESTIONNAIRE

491) **C.**
This information, never supplied by Fleming, can be found in Pearson's biography of 007 (see answer 483). Supposedly, James Bond was born in a town called Wattenscheid, near Essen in Germany. His father was

working there at the time, so his mother was unable to return to England for the birth.

492) **C.**
Armistice Day

493) **A.**
Andrew Bond was a Scot, born in Glencoe. Monique Dellacroix Bond was born in Canton de Vaud, Switzerland.

494) **B.**
They both fell while climbing a mountain near Aiguilles Rouges, near Chamonix.

495) **B.**
Bond had an elder brother named Henry, and Aunt Charmain looked after the two of them after their parents were killed.

496) **A.**
Commander James Bond, "Companion of the Order of St. Michael and St. George," Royal Navy Volunteer Reserve.

497) **FALSE.**
When he left Kissy Suzuki at the end of *YOU ONLY LIVE TWICE,* the Ama island girl was pregnant. In 1963, she bore him a son, and without a father around to give him a last name, she named the boy James Suzuki. According to the legend, Bond visited the boy and even took him to visit Glencoe, Scotland. Kissy married a Japanese man who worked for Shell Oil, and they raised the boy as their own.

498) **A.**
This was what Bond was earning in 1955, as recorded in Fleming's *MOONRAKER* novel.

499) **A.**
While it seems like this number should be larger, a careful read through every one of Fleming's stories will bear this fact out.

500) **C.**
While 007 has undoubtedly been indirectly responsible for the death of hundreds of men and women, he has personally killed (in some manner)

only 130 people in the Eon Productions films. But let's not be hard on the guy—after all, he has saved the world from disaster and destruction many times over. Of course, anyone else with this track record would have been thrown in jail (and probably executed) long ago. But the numbers weigh heavily in his—and our—favor. . . . Keep up the good work, Mr. Bond.

APPENDIX

James Bond books written by Ian Fleming:

CASINO ROYALE (1953)
LIVE AND LET DIE (1954)
MOONRAKER (1955)
DIAMONDS ARE FOREVER (1956)
FROM RUSSIA WITH LOVE (1957)
DOCTOR NO (1958)
GOLDFINGER (1959)
FOR YOUR EYES ONLY (1960)
THUNDERBALL (1961)
THE SPY WHO LOVED ME (1962)
ON HER MAJESTY'S SECRET SERVICE (1963)
YOU ONLY LIVE TWICE (1964)
THE MAN WITH THE GOLDEN GUN (1965)
OCTOPUSSY (1966)

Other books written by Ian Fleming:

THE DIAMOND SMUGGLERS (1957)
THRILLING CITIES (1963)
CHITTY CHITTY BANG BANG (1964)

James Bond books written by other authors:

COLONEL SUN (1968)
    By Robert Markham (alias Kingsley Amis)

JAMES BOND—THE AUTHORIZED BIOGRAPHY OF 007 (1973)
  By John Pearson
THE SPY WHO LOVED ME (1977)
  By Christopher Wood (movie tie-in)
JAMES BOND AND MOONRAKER (1979)
  By Christopher Wood (movie tie-in)
LICENSE RENEWED (1981)
  By John Gardner
FOR SPECIAL SERVICES (1982)
  By John Gardner
ICEBREAKER (1983)
  By John Gardner

THE JAMES BOND FILMS

DOCTOR NO (1962)
  Produced by Harry Saltzman and Albert R. Broccoli (Eon
    Productions)
  Directed by Terence Young
  Screenplay by Richard Maibaum, Johanna Harwood and Berkely
    Mather
  From the novel by Ian Fleming
  Music composed by Monty Norman, orchestrated by Burt Rhodes
  James Bond Theme played by the John Barry Orchestra
  Production Designer: Ken Adam
  Editor: Peter Hunt
  Distributed by United Artists, 106 minutes.
FROM RUSSIA WITH LOVE (1963)
  Produced by Harry Saltzman and Albert R. Broccoli (Eon
    Productions)
  Directed by Terence Young
  Screenplay by Richard Maibaum, Johanna Harwood
  From the novel by Ian Fleming
  Title song written by Lionel Bart
  Orchestral music composed and conducted by John Barry
  Art Director: Syd Cain
  Editor: Peter Hunt
  Distributed by United Artists, 116 minutes
GOLDFINGER (1964)
  Produced by Harry Saltzman and Albert R. Broccoli (Eon
    Productions)

Directed by Guy Hamilton
Screenplay by Richard Maibaum and Paul Dehn
From the novel by Ian Fleming
Title song lyrics by Leslie Bricusse and Anthony Newley
Music composed and conducted by John Barry
Production Designer: Ken Adam
Editor: Peter Hunt
Distributed by United Artists, 109 minutes

THUNDERBALL (1965)
Produced by Kevin McClory
Directed by Terence Young
Screenplay by Richard Maibaum and John Hopkins
Based on an original screenplay by Jack Whittingham, Kevin
McClory and Ian Fleming
"Thunderball" lyrics by Don Black
Music composed and conducted by John Barry
Production Designer: Ken Adam
Supervising Editor: Peter Hunt
Distributed by United Artists, 125 minutes

CASINO ROYALE (1967)
Produced by Charles K. Feldman and Jerry Bresler
Directed by John Huston, Ken Hughes, Val Guest, Robert Parrish
and Joe McGrath
Screenplay by Wolf Mankowitz, John Law and Michael Sayers
Suggested by Ian Fleming's novel, *CASINO ROYALE*
Lyrics by Hal David
Music by Burt Bacharach
Editor: Bill Lenny
Columbia Pictures release of a Famous Artists Production, 131
minutes

YOU ONLY LIVE TWICE (1967)
Produced by Harry Saltzman and Albert R. Broccoli (Eon-Danjaq)
Directed by Lewis Gilbert
Screenplay by Roald Dahl
Title Song lyrics by Leslie Bricusse
Music composed, conducted and arranged by John Barry
Production Designer: Ken Adam
Editor: Thelma Cornell
Distributed by United Artists, 116 minutes

ON HER MAJESTY'S SECRET SERVICE (1969)
Produced by Harry Saltzman and Albert R. Broccoli (Eon-Danjaq)

Directed by Peter Hunt
Screenplay by Richard Maibaum
Lyrics by Hal David
Music by John Barry
Production Designer: Syd Cain
Editor and Second Unit Director: John Glen
Distributed by United Artists, 140 minutes

DIAMONDS ARE FOREVER (1971)

Produced by Harry Saltzman and Albert R. Broccoli (Eon Productions)
Directed by Guy Hamilton
Screenplay by Richard Maibaum and Tom Mankiewicz
Lyrics by Don Black
Music by John Barry
Production Designer: Ken Adam
Editors: Bert Bates and John W. Holmes, A.C.E.
Distributed by United Artists, 119 minutes

LIVE AND LET DIE (1973)

Produced by Harry Saltzman and Albert R. Broccoli (Eon Productions)
Directed by Guy Hamilton
Screenplay by Tom Mankiewicz
Title song by Paul and Linda McCartney
Music by George Martin
Supervising Art Director: Syd Cain
Editors: Bert Bates, Raymond Poulton and John Shirley
Distributed by United Artists, 121 minutes

THE MAN WITH THE GOLDEN GUN (1974)

Produced by Harry Saltzman and Albert R. Broccoli (Eon Productions)
Directed by Guy Hamilton
Screenplay by Richard Maibaum and Tom Mankiewicz
Lyrics by Don Black
Music by John Barry
Production Designer: Peter Murton
Supervising Editor: John Shirley
Distributed by United Artists, 125 minutes

THE SPY WHO LOVED ME (1977)

Produced by Albert R. Broccoli (Eon Productions)
Directed by Lewis Gilbert
Screenplay by Christopher Wood and Richard Maibaum

Lyrics by Carole Bayer Sager
Music composed by Marvin Hamlisch
Production Designer: Ken Adam
Editor: John Glen
Distributed by United Artists, 125 minutes

MOONRAKER (1979)

Produced by Albert R. Broccoli (Eon-Les Productions Artistes Associés)
Directed by Lewis Gilbert
Screenplay by Christopher Wood
Executive Producer: Michael G. Wilson
Lyrics by Hal David
Music by John Barry
Production Designer: Ken Adam
Editor: John Glen
Distributed by United Artists, 126 minutes

FOR YOUR EYES ONLY (1981)

Produced by Albert R. Broccoli (Eon Productions-Danjaq S.A.)
Directed by John Glen
Screenplay by Richard Maibaum and Michael G. Wilson
Executive Producer: Michael G. Wilson
Lyrics by Michael Leeson
Music by Bill Conti
Production Designer: Peter Lamont
Editor: John Grover
Distributed by United Artists, 127 minutes

OCTOPUSSY (1983)

Produced by Albert R. Broccoli (Eon Productions-Danjaq S.A.)
Directed by John Glen
Screen story and Screenplay by George MacDonald Fraser, Richard Maibaum and Michael G. Wilson
Executive Producer: Michael G. Wilson
Lyrics by Tim Rice
Music by John Barry
Production Designer: Peter Lamont
Supervising Editor: John Grover
Distributed by United Artists, 130 minutes

NEVER SAY NEVER AGAIN (1983)

Produced by Jack Schwartzman
Directed by Irvin Kershner
Screenplay by Lorenzo Semple, Jr.

Based on an original story by Kevin McClory, Jack Whittingham and
   Ian Fleming
Executive Producer: Kevin McClory
Lyrics by Alan and Marilyn Bergman
Music by Michel Legrand
Production Designer: Philip Harrison and Stephen Grimes
Supervising Film Editor: Robert Lawrence
Warner Brothers release of a Taliafilm Production, in Association
   with Producers Sales Organization, 137 minutes.

PHOTO CREDITS